CHILDREN'S DRAWI

Children's Drawings

(Le Dessin Enfantin)

Georges-Henri Luquet

Translated with an Introduction and Notes by
Alan Costall

FREE ASSOCIATION BOOKS / LONDON / NEW YORK

First published in Great Britain 2001 by
Free Association Books
57 Warren Street
London W1T 5NR

www.fa-b.com

First published in 1927. Fifth edition published as *Le Dessin Enfantin* by
Delachaux et Niestlé © 1991

ISBN 1 85343 516 3 pbk

A CIP catalogue record for this book is available from the British Library

Designed and produced for Free Association Books Ltd by
Chase Publishing Services, Fortescue, Sidmouth EX10 9QG
Printed in the European Union by Antony Rowe, Chippenham, England

Contents

Introduction: A Closer Look at Luquet by Alan Costall vii

PART 1 THE ELEMENTS OF CHILDREN'S DRAWINGS

1 The Intention 3

2 The Interpretation 18

3 The Type 31

4 The Internal Model 47

5 Use of Colour 65

PART 2 THE DEVELOPMENT OF CHILDREN'S DRAWINGS

6 Realism 77

7 First Stage: Fortuitous Realism 85

8 Second Stage: Failed Realism 93

9 Third Stage: Intellectual Realism 102

10 Graphic Narration 129

Conclusions: Psychological and Educational 141

Short Bibliography 161

Glossary of Key Terms by Alan Costall 162

Index 167

Introduction
A Closer Look at Luquet

Alan Costall

Georges-Henri Luquet was born at Rochefort-sur-Mer on 23 January 1876. His interests were remarkably wide. He published works on mediaeval history, on logic and philosophy, and on anthropology (he had studied with both Henri Bergson and Lucien Lévy-Bruhl). He also made contributions to general psychology, and was a leading figure in La Société Française de Psychology, and a contributor to the *Journal de Psychologie*. He became a Mason in 1906, and devoted much of his later life to researching the history of French Masonry. He lived a long and full life, and died on 4 November 1965.[1]

Luquet is mainly remembered as a developmental psychologist by English readers, and primarily for the present work, *Le Dessin Enfantin*, published in 1927. In fact, he published a large number of texts and articles on children's drawings, and also on prehistoric and primitive art (e.g. Luquet, 1930a and 1930b). His first book on children's drawings, *Les Dessins d'un Enfant*, was published in 1913, and remains one of the most intensive and sensitive studies of a child and her drawings. The book was based on his own daughter, Simonne, born in 1904, and includes 1687 of her drawings, precisely dated and often accompanied by carefully observed information about what she was doing and saying at the time.

> I have not in fact seen any example of a monographic study [i.e. a study based on direct observation] which, either in the duration of the observations or its minute attention to detail, approximates the care I devoted to the drawings of my daughter, Simonne. Indeed, even though I was already trained in this kind of study by this initial work, I myself was unable to resume the study with her younger brother [born in 1906], mainly because of lack of time to observe him so closely and continuously. (Luquet, 1922, pp. 212–13)

At the time, there was a positive frenzy for amassing vast collections of drawings, usually through the help of school teachers, but the researchers seldom had anything to do with the children themselves. As Luquet noted, such studies provide very little information about the actual children who produced the drawings (little more than their age and gender), and so the data deriving from them are of limited scientific value. Furthermore, he argued, such drawings were not spontaneous, the subjects for the drawings being imposed upon the children, and so studies based upon them give a distorted impression of what children would draw if left to themselves. Luquet had similar misgivings about experimental studies (the favoured method in modern psychology):

> One resorts to experimentation when obervation does not yield the facts necessary for the study, that is, when the subject, placed in normal conditions, does not act in the way we would wish. Consequently, the conditions under which the subject is then placed by the experimenter are abnormal, at least for that subject. The subject is thereby deformed by experimentation, so that when observed on a later occasion one cannot be sure that the results we obtain from him would conform to those which we would have found if he had not been subjected to experiment earlier. (Luquet, 1922, p. 218)

Luquet was convinced that his main approach – the method of direct observation or 'monographic study' – was the most appropriate for understanding the psychology of children's drawings.[2] However, he was well aware that the investigator had to proceed with caution, taking care, for example, not to become too intrusive or conspicuous. The main limitation of studies based on single cases is that of generalisation: is the child typical of other children? In the present work, Luquet sought to collate evidence from different studies to identify common trends in the development of drawing.

Despite the heroic demands of his intensive study of his own daughter's drawings, Luquet retained his enthusiasm and wonder at their remarkable inventiveness. As a nice touch, *Les Dessins d'un Enfant* includes a signed photograph of Simonne to precede the collection of her many drawings. The style of the present work, *Le Dessin Enfantin*, is more 'impersonal', and when Luquet refers to his own children, he refers to them rather anonymously as Simonne L. and Jean L.[3] It is as though he is trying to reassure the reader about his scientific detachment. Nevertheless, although Luquet has often been mistaken for a very orthodox theorist, he is in many ways a dissident figure. His work radically challenges the conventional wisdom about children's drawings, not least by taking children and their drawings seriously.

The 'Sensory Core' and the 'Innocent Eye'

The scientific 'discovery' of children was relatively recent and remarkably sudden, and can be located mainly to the 1880s. The reasons for this are in part theoretical, such as the rise of evolutionism and its emphasis on origins and transformation, but also economic and political, with the increasing isolation of children from the world of work, and the creation of 'childhood' as a world of its own.

Along with the existence of children, investigators also came to take note of their drawings. The Italian art critic and historian, Corrado Ricci, one of the earliest writers on children's drawings, not only located his 'discovery' to a specific place and day (during the winter of 1882–1883), but also managed to imply that it was indeed a surprise, comparable, perhaps, to the truly suprising discoveries of prehistoric cave art occurring at that time:

> I was driven by a downpour of rain to take refuge under the portico leading to Meloncello. I had not known that under this arch was to be found a permanent exhibition, both literary and artistic, possessing little aesthetic merit perhaps, and hardly what could be considered chaste. The works of the youngest artists, those occurring, naturally, lowest down on the wall, showed themselves least technical and logical; they were, nevertheless, characterized by greater decency, and the poetical effusions were notably diminished. (Corrado Ricci, 1887. Translation taken from Barnes, 1894, p. 302.)

By the 1890s, many articles and books began to appear on children's drawings. One of the first English writers on the topic was James Sully, Professor of Mind and Logic at University College London. Sully devoted an extensive chapter of his classic text, *Studies of Childhood* (Sully, 1895/2000), to 'the young draughtsman'. Sully certainly conveys a delight in children's drawings, but he also helped to consolidate a theoretical approach that has continued to the present day. Sully framed 'the problem' of children's drawings in essentially negative terms. As he admitted, 'I have dwelt on what from our grown-up standpoint we must call the *defects* of children's drawings' (Sully, 1895, p. 396; emphasis added). As Sully saw it, the basic theoretical problem was to explain how it could be that children – *of all people* – should *fail* to draw in perspective. Mere lack of skill, he argued, could not be the fundamental explanation, since it was clear to any attentive observer that children were not *trying* to draw in perspective. But why were they not even trying?

Sully was committed to an assumption that has dominated Western theories of vision for many centuries, one so ingrained it seems to count as an indisputable fact of nature. This is the idea that there exists a 'sensory core', a primary level of visual experience that is perspectival and depthless (Costall, 1993 and 1994; Hatfield and Epstein, 1979). The sensory core is supposed to be primary not only in providing the raw data for higher-level intellectual processing, but also primitive in the developmental sense:

> Many suppose that the infant, if he distinguishes at all any individual visible thing, sees 'all objects as if painted upon a flat surface' – that he has as yet no conception of anything external, existing outside of his eye. (Preyer, 1888, p. 60)[4]

Why then does the child artist, if true to this primitive level of visual experience, *not* draw in immaculate perspective? The explanation offered by Sully closely follows earlier accounts provided by, among others, Helmholtz, Ruskin, and Ricci:

> ... the child's eye at a surprisingly early period loses its primal *'innocence,'* grows 'sophisticated' in the sense that instead of seeing what is really presented[,] it sees, or pretends to see, what knowledge and logic tell it is there. In other words his sense-perceptions have for artistic purposes become *corrupted* by a too large admixture of intelligence. (Sully, 1895, p. 396; emphases added)

Many years ago, the Gestalt psychologist, Rudolph Arnheim (1947), published a searching critique of such 'intellectualistic' theories of the development and history of art. He argued that it was the commitment of most theorists to the notion of the 'innocent eye' that led them (indeed, forced them) to suppose: (i) that it was solely deviations from perspective that required explanation, and (ii) that such deviations were to be explained not in terms of perception but the intervention of higher mental processes.[5]

One can envisage, and indeed discover, a variety of theories of this kind, differing in just two basic respects – the timing of the supposed process of cognitive intervention, and its exact nature. Given the actual logic of these so-called stage theories, they have proved highly flexible (not to say slippery) in explaining the facts, and a rich resource for those wishing to disparage the artistic efforts of others. They could accommodate the *appearance* of perspective *ad hoc* at any point in cultural history or individual development.

On the one hand, the artists of Classical Greece could be dismissed as immature precisely because of their *failure* to utilise a fixed perspective. These artists evidently had *still* not managed to control the corrupting effects of conceptual thought (Loewy, 1907). On the other hand, the use of perspective could also be taken as a sign of immaturity. Thus, as Karl Bühler (1930) noted, were the child somehow to become able to engage in drawing *before* the onset of the corrupting effect of language, the resulting drawings should presumably appear in more or less accurate perspective (cf. Lowenfeld, 1952, p. 138). Indeed, Bühler, along with other writers, such as Verworn (1917), Lowenfeld (1951) and Willcox (1984), also applied this logic to what they deemed to be grown-up children. They regarded the remarkable pictures of the palaeolithic artists or of the modern African bushmen, with their use of perspective and foreshortening, not as a sign of skill but of childishness, the retention of 'juvenile characteristics in adult life' (Willcox, 1984, p. 256). Here is Bühler's summary of Verworn's position:

> the realistic drawings of these primitive peoples are not to be regarded as the result of long practice and a well-kept tradition, but as the expression of a mind whose original talent for drawing had remained unspoilt. (Bühler, 1930, p. 123)

Many theorists of children's drawing have invoked intellectual factors, such as linguistic symbolism or abstract thought (e.g. Sully, 1895; Bühler, 1930) to explain how the innocent vision of the child comes to be repressed in their drawings; others have instead pointed to non-intellectual factors, such as tactile experience or emotional engagement with the object (Lowenfeld, 1951 and 1952; Werner, 1948, pp. 148–9).

In recent years, this pervasive explanatory schema of the repression of the innocent eye or sensory core has had a new lease of life in relation to examples of exceptional artistic ability shown by certain children with autism, such as Nadia Chomyn. Lorna Selfe, one of the first to research this intriguing topic, eventually came to make appeal to the concept of the innocent eye (e.g. Selfe, 1983, p. 86), explicitly drawing upon Bühler's theoretical work. There would seem to be a very broad consensus on the most likely explanation of such remarkable examples of precocious drawing ability (e.g. Arnheim, 1980; Pariser, 1981; Winner, 1982; Thomas and Silk, 1989, p. 138; Cox, 1992, p. 201; Snyder and Thomas, 1997). Here is Winner's formulation of the basic idea:

> ... Nadia's conceptual deficiency left her free to see and record objects with a naked eye. Nadia drew [as she did] precisely because people's visual concepts [normally] interfere with their photographic transcriptions. (Winner, 1982, p. 187)[6]

This explanation can also be found repeated by authors who, in many respects, are among the most searching critics of traditional theorising in child art. Thus we find David Pariser subscribing to the more familiar cognitive variant of the schema of perceptual innocence:

> Nadia inhabited a ... nameless, unlabelled universe, one which she saw and was able to render with phenomenal clarity without truly 'knowing.' ... Nadia's capacity for representational realism was, in part, the result of her inability or refusal to conceptualize what she drew. (Pariser, 1981, p. 20)

Arnheim, true to his early critique of 'the intellectualist theory', did not invoke a cognitive account of Nadia's impressive drawings. The explanation he offers is nevertheless a version of the same schema of innocence. Nadia, he argued, could access a state of 'pure vision' because of her inability to engage practically with objects:

> Given [the] barrier between [Nadia] and her surroundings one can imagine that many things of this world appeared to her not as challenges and tasks but as mere images, to be passively explored rather than actively responded to. Therefore she recorded what

she saw with something like the faithfulness of a photographic lens. (Arnheim, 1980, p. 85)[7]

In the modern literature, these early theories of the development of drawing are often described as 'stage theories', but this is profoundly misleading. These theories certainly were not claiming that perspectival representation could *never* occur early in development, nor were they suggesting that children's drawings were the *precondition* for the development of perspectival representation. The use of perspective does not, on these accounts, *develop from* an earlier stage. Indeed, in a fundamental sense, it does *not* develop at all. According to this dominant theoretical scheme, the ability to see and draw in perspective is present from the outset. It is simply 'held back' – repressed or 'inhibited' by extraneous factors, most notably by the development of conceptual thought and its corrupting effect on the innocent, perspectival vision of the child.[8]

Luquet on 'Intellectual Realism'

In much of the literature on children's drawings, Luquet's contribution has become reduced to a mere caption, 'Children draw what they *know*, and not what they *see*.'[9] As I have tried to explain, the distinction between *intellectual* and *visual* realism (if not the terminology) was well established before Luquet published his work.[10] Furthermore, although this distinction is indeed central to the present book, Luquet handles it in a way that distinguishes him from most other writers on children's drawings before or since. It is true that Luquet does follow the standard line of theorising in many important respects, but his sympathetic attitude to children's drawings, and various claims he makes about them, are ultimately subversive.[11]

Developmental researchers who base their work on observations of their own children are usually very sensitive to the charge of being too attached to the 'subjects' under study, and hence lacking in scientific objectivity. As I have already noted, Luquet in the present book seems to go out of his way to conceal the fact that much of the material is based on his own children. Yet 'close' study of children has obvious and unique advantages. It yields a wealth of detail, and particular events can be related to the life of the child. But there is also the question of *care*. Luquet's intensive study of his young daughter persisted for several years, and there was his doctorate at stake. There was always the risk that Simonne might become resentful of the attention or simply lose interest in drawing, and for Luquet himself it must have been hard work. His study could have easily degenerated into a mechanical, detached catalogue of her drawings. Fortunately, Luquet cared for his child at least as much as his Ph.D. He remained open to the meaning and creativity of her work, and this enabled him to think differently about the nature of children's drawings.

The first way in which Luquet stands out from most other theorists is that he does not regard intellectual realism as a failure. Nothing is 'stopping' children from drawing in perspective. They are not passive victims of some inhibitory force. Their own distinctive way of drawing is their *choice*. Although children are not 'realists' in the sense of producing a perspectival likeness of things, they are attempting to produce faithfully detailed representations of objects 'in themselves'.[12] The child opts primarily for intellectual realism, because 'what matters to the child is not the appearance an object takes from a contingent, variable viewpoint' (Luquet, this volume, p. 150)', but the persisting properties of that object, and its practical significance.

In addition to defining intellectual realism in terms of its distinct purpose for the child artist, Luquet also attempted to define it, at a more theoretical level, in terms of how children's drawings are 'generated'. According to Luquet, children's drawings are not based on the visual appearance of the object as such, but on an 'internal model', the child's mental representation of the entire object. Now the internal model serves two distinct functions in Luquet's acount. The first is to explain why children's drawings are selective in the details they include. The second is to account for the fact that children do *not* draw in perspective. But, somehow, Luquet simply forgets to provide an explanation of precisely how the internal model is supposed to generate the kinds of out-of-perspective drawings children actually produce. He simply talks of the drawings being 'translations' on paper of the internal model. But, of course, the internal model is supposed to be a representation of the object in its *entirety* (it is an object-centred representation, to use more modern terminology). It could not literally be 'copied' onto paper. Yet at several points in the present work, Luquet *identifies* the structure of the internal model with the distinctive structure – the 'type' – of the child's actual drawing, the one simply being the external manifestation of the other. In this respect, the internal model ends up doing no serious explanatory work at all.[13] It simply internalises, rather than solves, the fundamental and general problem of pictorial representation: how to represent a richly structured and changing world on a two-dimensional, unchanging surface.

If indeed the concept of the internal model were really so fundamental to Luquet's theory, then his failure to explain precisely how it is supposed to 'work' would be fatal, and render his account of children's drawings of mere historical interest. But accompanying his conventional, cognitive account of intellectual realism, there is an important 'sub-text'.

As it happens, Luquet *does* provide an alternative and perfectly adequate account of the forms that children's drawings actually take, but in terms of a whole array of distinctive *drawing techniques,* such as 'transparency' (showing otherwise occluded details), and 'rabattement' (folding out the sides of an object, as it were, to reveal them on the paper). He thereby undermines the very idea that intellectual realism might be envisaged as a unified and coherent 'system' comparable to the (idealised) notion of linear perspective as a monolithic system.[14] What ultimately holds intellectual realism together, in Luquet's account, is not a generative cognitive 'mechanism', but an aspiration: the intention, on the part of the child, to represent objects or events in their entirety.

But Luquet goes further still. Without seeming to notice the theoretical havoc he is causing, he manages to detach the concept of intellectual realism from the dominant theoretical *opposition* between seeing and knowing.[15] Admittedly, Luquet never seriously questions the *conceptual* basis of *intellectual* realism (as I have noted, he is curiously negligent about that side of his theory). What he challenges, instead, is the *perceptual* basis of *visual* realism. And the effect is just as devastating.

Luquet's first book on children's drawings was published in 1913, the year of the first cubist manifestos, and it is tantalising that even in his later 1927 text he makes no reference to cubism. For there are intriguing similarities. The early manifestos not only stress the artificiality and contingency of the frozen, perspectival view, they also propose that the new form of painting is actually closer to our normal visual experience, given that we are not static, one-eyed creatures but perpetually on the move.[16] Unlike the cubists, Luquet *never* goes so far as to claim that intellectual realism is the 'real' *visual* realism. However, he does question the 'informativeness' of the 'contingent, variable viewpoint' of visual realism, and indeed insists that children have *good reason* to have misgivings about its limitations (p. 150). He also denies its 'naturalness', arguing that visual realism is as much a convention as intellectual realism (see p. 156). As he puts it, the relation between intellectual and visual realism is analogous to that between different 'idioms' of verbal languages (p. 156; Luquet, 1913, p. 248).[17] In short, he blatantly denies linear perspective the naturalistic rationale that has been so fundamental to the majority of theories of children's drawings, then and since. Linear perspective, he insists, has no compelling justification in the nature of visual experience. Appreciating the full significance of this move on Luquet's part is crucial to understanding the real point and essence of his overall theory. As I shall now explain, Luquet's theory is not a naturalistic, stage theory in its treatment of the relation between intellectual and visual realism; it is not really a naturalistic theory at all. And his work involves a profound *re-evaluation* of children drawings, or, more precisely, of their *ideal* of what a drawing should be.

Luquet and Stage Theory

Within developmental biology and psychology, the notion of 'stages' is linked (often implicitly) to the concept of progress, and to the idea of relatively abrupt transformations. Each developmental stage is supposed to give rise naturally to the next, with earlier stages being not only prior to – but inferior to – later stages. Up to a point, Luquet's theory seems to conform perfectly to that format. In the first stage, *fortuitous realism*, the child has absolutely no intention of creating a representation but enjoys making marks for their own sake. In the course of making meaningless traces, however, the child notices that sometimes the drawings can nevertheless resemble something else.[18] In the next stage, *failed realism*, the child, having made this discovery, deliberately attempts to produce actual representations but keeps failing through lack of drawing skill and also the inability to attend to, and hence relate, the different parts of the drawing. So far, Luquet's account very much accords with what we should expect from a stage theory. These first stages not only clearly 'lead' to one another, but they also involve a definite *advancement* in drawing. Yet even for these so-called stages, Luquet repeatedly warns that they do not involve any abrupt transitions nor do they ultimately displace one another. For example, an older child or even an adult may engage in meaningless scribbling, and a child who has progressed beyond failed realism in relation to certain drawings may have difficulties all over again when taking on a new subject.

It is from the point where children have finally managed to get their act together, that Luquet's account takes a quite different turn. Beyond the stage of failed realism, the child is now ready and able to produce realistic drawings, but is faced with a dilemma: whether to opt for visual realism or intellectual realism given that *both* options have their limitations. Intellectual realism can be inclusive and relate all salient features and surfaces to the object to which they belong. A cube, for example, can be depicted by showing all its sides – even the far side – folded out onto the paper. Its limitation (one quickly encountered by the cubists) is that it is impossible to connect all of the parts of an object *to one another*. It cannot, for example, show how *all* the sides of a cube connect to one another. Linear perspective, on the other hand, inevitably excludes many of the features of the object depicted, and does so in what may seem to be an arbitrary way. What it *can* do, however, is relate those limited aspects of the object shown in the picture to one another. As Luquet explains, a similar dilemma also occurs in the depiction of events given that, once more, both visual and intellectual realism each have their own limitations, this time in conveying either continuity or change (see his chapter on 'graphic narration', and also Luquet, 1924).

The young child *chooses* intellectual realism. To an extent, Luquet offers a naturalistic explanation for that choice. From a biological point of view, he argues, children should be concerned not with the contingent and transient aspects of things but with their practical significance, and the biological function of an object depends upon the entire object. Nevertheless, nothing 'causes' the child to be an intellectual realist. To repeat, the child, according to Luquet, makes a choice, and this choice is both reasonable and informed. Normally, children soon become aware of the existence of perspective representations, but they do not themselves choose to draw that way because of what they regard as its serious limitations.

The relation between intellectual and visual realism is not, therefore, one between 'stages' in the standard sense. Luquet's account, ultimately, invokes reasons rather than causes. Intellectual realism is not something the child 'undergoes' as a preliminary to visual realism. It reflects a 'reasonable' commitment to an alternative *ideal* of what a drawing should be.

Although, in Luquet's account, children are eventually won over to the virtues of linear perspective, this involves no ultimate and categorical transition between 'stages'. Intellectual and visual realism are not distinct developmental 'states'. They are contrasting ideals, and they can coexist in the same child (or indeed adult) and even be realised together in the same drawing.[19] First of all, as Luquet was well aware, very young children may sometimes produce pictures in very stark perspective (such as extreme foreshortening, as in figure 136),[20] and adults, even within Western cultures, resort to some of the devices of intellectual realism. Secondly, in practice, the distinction between intellectual and visual realism is not always so very profound. As Luquet put it, there can be 'conciliation between the two realisms' (Luquet, 1930a, p. 94; see also sections 9 and 47 of the present work). When taking a photograph, for example, we do not just open the shutter randomly and hope for the best. We take care to position ourselves in relation to the subject to maximise the available information. In many cases, timing is also important, as when taking someone's portrait. In short, we select an *intelligent* perspective. Now this is what Luquet believed children are also doing in their deployment of 'exemplarity', where the individual surfaces and features of an object are given their most distinctive and informative shapes. But in this case, there is a mixture of perspectives, each part of the object being 'viewed' from its own optimal viewpoint (for some nice examples, see figures 111, 116, and 121). 'Change of point of view', in space and also time, is thereby a compromise between visual and intellectual realism:

> There is visual realism [locally] because the eye and instantaneous photography can register an image similar to the drawing, and also intellectual realism, since the [object] is represented in its entirety. (Luquet, 1930a, p. 92)

What, however, ultimately distances Luquet's account of intellectual and visual realism most clearly from traditional stage theory is the fact that he does not regard the final stage of development, the adoption of visual realism, as an unqualified *advance*. He does not consider that there is anything ultimately 'wrong' or essentially childish about intellectual realism.[21]

The *Value* of Child Art

Luquet concludes the present book with a discussion of drawing in relation to children's education. He argues that the child should not be discouraged from employing intellectual realism since it encourages a keen sense of observation. As a way of teaching the child about things themselves, 'intellectual realism is infinitely preferable since it involves precisely the reproduction of all the details, each in its proper shape, so that the child becomes engaged in a kind of spontaneous dissection of the object' (p. 157).

Yet it was not simply for its educational value that Luquet believed that we should take intellectual realism much more seriously. He was genuinely fascinated by the surprising resources (or to use a more recent term, 'affordances') of this alternative mode of representation.[22] He was astonished, for example, by the capacity of his daughter to represent events or narratives, not by the depiction of characteristic instants or by the technique of the comic strip, but by setting out the various successive positions of the changing event on the same unchanging background. Intellectual realism, he concluded, is a remarkable system. It is no more (or less) a convention than visual realism, and has its own definite advantages:

> Intellectual realism allows the child's drawing to be at the same time a sort of flat sculpture in its representation of space (even if sculpture, unlike the child's drawings, is not transparent), and a kind of miniature theatre in its representation of time. It is thus, in a certain way, a universal art, and one that deserves serious attention before we try to dismiss it. (p. 156; see also Luquet, 1913, p. 250)

Luquet also reminds us of the important fact that 'we find engineers, mechanics, and designers mixing in the same image different points of view, no less than the child (p. 156)'. He includes among his examples the use of plans and elevations by architects, and the double portraits (i.e. profile plus full-face) devised by Galton for the purposes of both physical anthropology and criminology. If modern adults continue to employ these techniques, Luquet insisted, it is surely not a question of 'regression', but because for adults, too, there is good reason. In short, Luquet evidently regarded intellectual realism not merely as a transitional or intrusive stage, but as a serious and enduring option. In fact, in his first book on children's drawings, he explicitly raised the interesting and (in relation to the contemporary developments in painting) timely question of what might arise if artists were to devote to intellectual realism the same care that they give to visual realism:

> Who knows, but we might be faced with a completely different art yet one able to produce equivalent effects by quite different means. This is only an hypothesis, but one which could be put to an exact test if it should seem worthwhile. (Luquet, 1913, p. 248)

Notes

1. For further biographical details about Luquet and a full bibliography of his work, see Caroff, Giraud, Soyez, and Thoumy (1970–1971). See also Lurçat (1972–1973).
2. Luquet also used the 'method of graffiti', namely the study of drawings children scrawl on walls and other surfaces (see Luquet, 1922). The virtue of such drawings for research is that they are spontaneous. An obvious limitation is that it is normally difficult to obtain information about the children themselves. A further problem, as Luquet noted, is that a grown-up going around earnestly tracing copies of graffiti can arouse suspicion from both the children themselves and other adults.
3. In my translation, I have restored their surnames.
4. Strictly speaking, this primitive experience should not be of flatness, but of 'depthlessness'. As Merleau-Ponty (1964, p. 65) has noted, the experience of flatness itself presupposes a definite spatial location, and hence an awareness of depth.
5. A different and completely contrasting notion of 'the innocent eye' has been influential within art education, where it is the child's non-perspectival art that is regarded as 'innocent' and it is the imposition of perspective on the child by the adult world that is the 'corruption'. See Costall (1997) for a comparison of these contrasting schemas of innocence and corruption.
6. The idea that such precocious ability is merely a 'symptom' of autism, the automatic 'release' of an inherent capacity to see and draw in perspective, does not bear close examination (see Costall, 1997). Such exceptional artistic ability is very rare among children with autism. It can occur among children with no obvious impairments in language or symbolism; the ability does not arise 'just like that' but is a skill based on the careful study of other pictures, and the drawings themselves have an individual style, and specialise in particular topics, such as animals or buildings.
7. Curiously, Arnheim fails to note that, in a most obvious way, Nadia did engage exceptionally well with objects, namely when she used pens and paper to create her drawings.

8. In the nineteenth century, the physiological concept of inhibition (the idea that neural activity could have a suppressive rather than excitatory effect) had a profound impact on psychological theory, most notably Freudian theory. Verworn, one of the early writers on child and 'primitive' art, was himself a physiologist working on neural inhibition (Smith, 1992, p. 139).
9. Informative accounts of Luquet's work can be found in Read (1943) and Freeman (1972).
10. Luquet himself initially used the term 'logical' rather than 'intellectual' realism: 'For the child, a picture counts as a good likeness if it includes all the actual features of the object, all its logical elements ...' (Luquet, 1913, p. 186).
11. Luquet's contemporaries, even such astute critics as Henri Wallon and Maurice Merleau-Ponty, do not seem to have appreciated this. They regarded his treatment of children's drawings as both overly static and dismissive (see Caroff et al., 1970–1971).
12. In adopting the term 'intellectual realism' to describe young children's drawings, Luquet was placing as much emphasis on the *realism* of children's drawings, to make a contrast with symbolism and schematism.
13. Recent attempts to deploy Luquet's concept of the internal model have made a connection with David Marr's distinction between viewer-centred and object-centred representations (Marr, 1982). But it is important to be clear that children's drawings are not – and could not – *themselves* be object-centred representations in Marr's sense.
14. Linear perspective is not, and never has been, a unified system *in practice*. Historically, it has always involved the piecemeal deployment of specific techniques, and its use has been subject to very definite constraints: e.g. the avoidance of wide-angle views, and 'awkward' viewpoints (see Pirenne, 1970).
15. Arnheim expresses what is wrong with the supposed opposition of seeing and knowing in a beautifully clear way: 'Now knowledge has more than one meaning. Much picture-making does not in fact rely on what the eyes happen to see at the moment the picture is produced. Instead the draftsman relies on a synthesis of his many previous observations of a certain kind of things, whether horses, trees, or human figures. This process can indeed be described as drawing from knowledge; but it is a knowledge that cannot be taken to be an alternative to seeing' (Arnheim, 1974, p. 164). See also Read (1943) for a similar critique of the 'conceptual fallacy'.
16. The later manifestos retreat from this position to the standard position that non-perspectival art is inherently conceptual (see Fry, 1978).
17. He also cites evidence that perspective images are not readily comprehensible to people unused to this system. However, much of the cross-cultural research on picture perception available in Luquet's time and long since has been flawed, even prejudiced (see Jones and Hagen, 1980). Certainly photographs and drawings in perspective are more accessible than Luquet supposed.

18. Luquet failed to note that children's earliest so-called scribbles can sometimes be representationally highly charged. In such cases, the child is concerned not with the marks left over, as it were, on the paper, but the act of mark-making itself. For example, the child may trace the swooping movements of a fighter-jet while making appropriate, if off-putting, noises. See the classic paper by John Matthews (1984) on such 'action representations'.
19. Rather than referring to biological or psychological stage theories, Luquet cites Comte's sociological law of the three stages of human society to emphasise that stages are not mutually exclusive. Comte's theory is not formulated at the level of the individual but of society.
20. Luquet also cites an example of visual realism in relation to a drawing by a girl as young as four years and three months. She drew a cat with just one ear and then explained 'Just one ear; the other cannot be seen' (see section 79).
21. A good deal of research effort has been exerted by developmental psychologists since the 1970s to challenge Luquet's account (and indeed 'stage theory' in general) by demonstrating that young children can (under appropriate laboratory conditions) draw in perspective (for reviews, see Freeman and Cox, 1985; Thomas and Silk, 1990; Cox, 1992). However, the fact that children may under appropriate conditions omit (rather than include) 'hidden' details of an object from their drawings (e.g., the occluded handle of a mug) does not in itself imply that they are able to draw 'in perspective' in any fuller sense of the word (see Costall, 1994). In any case, as I have tried to explain, Luquet was well aware of the appearance of visual realism in the drawings of young children (e.g. the omission of occluded features and indeed the use of foreshortening), and it is perfectly consistent with his view of the relation between intellectual and visual realism.
22. The term 'affordances' was coined by the psychologist, James Gibson (see Gibson, 1979).

References

Arnheim, R. (1947). Perceptual abstraction and art. *Psychological Review, 54*, 66–82.

Arnheim, R. (1974). *Art and visual perception.* (Revised edition.) Berkeley: University of California Press.

Arnheim, R. (1980). The puzzle of Nadia's drawings. *The Arts in Psychotherapy, 7*, 79–85.

Barnes, E. (1894). The art of little children. *Pedagogical Seminary, 3*, 302–7.

Bühler, K. (1930). *The mental development of the child.* London: Kegan Paul.

Caroff, A., Giraud, B., Soyez, S., and Thoumy, H. (1970–1971). G.H. Luquet et le dessin enfantin. *Bulletin de Psychologie, 24* (12–15), 743–70.

Costall, A. (1993). Beyond linear perspective: A cubist manifesto for visual science. *Image and Vision Computing, 11*, 334–41.

Costall, A. (1994). The myth of the sensory core: The traditional versus the ecological approach to children's drawings. In C. Lange-Kuettner and G.V. Thomas (eds), *Drawing and looking: Theoretical approaches to pictorial representation in children* (pp. 16–26). Hemel Hempstead: Harvester.

Costall, A. (1997). Innocence and corruption: Conflicting images of child art. *Human Development*, 40, 133–44.

Cox, M. (1992). *Children's drawings*. London: Penguin.

Freeman, N.H. (1972). Process and product in children's drawing. *Perception, 1*, 123–40.

Freeman, N.H. and Cox, M.V. (eds) (1985). *Visual order*. Cambridge: Cambridge University Press.

Fry, E.F. (1978). *Cubism*. New York: Oxford University Press.

Gibson, J.J. (1979). *The ecological approach to visual perception*. Boston: Houghton-Mifflin.

Hatfield, G.C. and Epstein, W. (1979). The sensory core and the medieval foundations of early modern perceptual theory. *ISIS, 70*, 363–84.

Jones, R., and Hagen, M. (1980). A perspective on cross-cultural picture perception. In M. Hagen (ed.), *The perception of pictures, Vol. II*. New York: Academic Press.

Loewy, E. (1907). *The rendering of nature in early Greek art* [trans. J. Fothergill]. London: Duckworth and Co. [First published in 1900.]

Lowenfeld, V. (1951). Psycho-aesthetic implications of the art of the blind, *Journal of Aesthetics and Art Criticism, 10 (1)*, 1–9.

Lowenfeld, V. (1952). *The nature of creative activity*. (2nd edn) London: Routledge and Kegan Paul.

Luquet, G.-H. (1913). *Les dessins d'un enfant: Thèse pour le doctorat presenté à la faculté des lettres de l'université de Lille*. Paris: Librarie Félix Alcan.

Luquet, G.-H. (1922). La méthode dans l'étude des dessins d'enfants. *Journal de Psychologie, 19*, 193–221. [English translation by Alan Costall available as: Method in the study of children's drawings, University of Southampton Research Working Papers, 1993, No. 30.]

Luquet, G.-H. (1924). La narration graphique chez l'enfant. *Journal de Psychologie, 21*, 183–218. [Translation by Alan Costall available as: Graphic narration in the child, University of Southampton Research Working Papers, 1993, No. 31.]

Luquet, G.-H. (1927). *Le dessin enfantin*. Paris: Alcan, 1927. [Fifth edition published in 1991 by Delachaux and Niestle (Lausanne and Paris), with introduction and commentary by J. Depouilly.]

Luquet, G.-H. (1930a). *The art and religion of fossil man*. New Haven : Yale University Press. [Translated by J.T. Russell from: *L'art et la religion des hommes fossiles*. Paris : Masson et Cie, 1926.]

Luquet, G.-H. (1930b). *L'art primitif*. Paris: Doin et Cie.

Lurçat, L. (1972–1973). Luquet et le dessin enfantin. *Bulletin de Psychologie, 26* (12–13).

Marr, D. (1982). *Vision*. San Francisco: W.H. Freeman.

Matthews, J. (1984). Children drawing: Are young children really scribbling? *Early Child Development and Care, 18*, 1–39.

Merleau-Ponty, M. (1964). *L'oeil et l'esprit*. Paris: Gallimard.

Pariser, D. (1981). Nadia's drawings: Theorizing about an autistic child's phenomenal ability. *Journal of Studies in Art Education, 22* (2), 20–9.

Pirenne, M.H. (1970). *Optics, painting and photography*. Cambridge: Cambridge University Press.

Preyer, W. (1888). *The mind of the child Part I: The senses and the will: observations concerning the mental life of the human being in the first years of life* [trans H.W. Brown]. New York: D. Appleton and Co. [Translation of 2nd edition, 1884; first edition, 1881.]

Read, H. (1943). *Education through art*. London: Faber and Faber.

Ricci, C. (1887). *L'arte dei bambini*. Bologna: Zanichelli, editore.

Selfe, L. (1983). *Normal and anomalous representational drawing ability in children*. London: Academic Press.

Smith, R. (1992). *Inhibition: History and meaning in the sciences of mind and brain*. Berkeley: University of California Press.

Snyder, A.W. and Thomas, M. (1997). Autistic artists give clues to cognition. *Perception, 26*, 93–6.

Sully, J. (1895). *Studies of childhood*. London: Longmans, Green. [The American edition of 1896 was reprinted in 2000 by Free Assocation Books (London and New York), with introductions by Susan Sugarman and Elizabeth Valentine.]

Thomas, G.V. and Silk, A.M.J. (1989). *An introduction to the psychology of children's drawings*. New York: Harvester Wheatsheaf.

Verworn, M. (1917). *Zur Psychologie der primitiven Kunst*. Jena: Fischer. (First published 1908.)

Werner, Heinz. (1948). *The comparative psychology of mental development*. [Rev. ed.] New York: International University Press.

Willcox, A.R. (1984). *The rock of art of Africa*. London: Croom Helm.

Winner, E. (1982). *Invented Worlds: the psychology of the arts*. Cambridge, MA: Harvard University Press.

PART 1

THE ELEMENTS OF CHILDREN'S DRAWINGS

1
The Intention[1]

1. Children draw for fun. For them, drawing is just like other games, and is interspersed among them. As has been observed for many different children, periods of graphic activity may be separated by intervals of several weeks or even months without any drawing, and it seems reasonable to conclude that their temporary disaffection with drawing may sometimes at least arise from dissatisfaction with their earlier efforts. There is no rigid formula to explain why at any given moment, and for a more or less lengthy period, children either prefer drawing to anything else, or come to abandon it. Nevertheless, one can say that it is a peaceful game, it does not require a partner, and it can be engaged in as easily indoors as outside. Thus, other things being equal, it will be those children with relatively calm temperaments who will prefer drawing, but all children will do so when they are alone, when they cannot play outside games or have become tired by them, or when they simply wish to engage in something new. In addition, drawing, like any other game, can take on a kind of obsessive quality, and be pursued for long periods at a time. A German boy of 13 months kept himself entertained by lifting and dropping the lid of a tankard. Another child, of 3 years, spent an hour and a quarter kneading some flour, salt and water, which he repeatedly transferred from one small pot to another, and when a stop was put to this game by removing the stick he had been using, he began to cry. Similarly, even young children, whose drawings still take the form of scribbles, have been observed keeping themselves amused in drawing for two or three hours at a stretch.

1. The later French editions of the book include some misprints. 'Coq' is printed instead of 'cop' in §19, 'sceau' instead of 'seau' in §30, and 'doit' instead of 'toit' in §64. Some text is missing from the final sentence of §20. In addition, important details are missing from figures 118 (a street lamp) and 133 (a second nose). These errors do not occur in the first edition, and have been corrected in this translation.

2. Furthermore, drawing is a game in which the child spontaneously applies the Kantian theory that disinterest is the distinctive quality of art: 'purposiveness without a purpose'.[2] Thus, a young girl of eight had drawn a sketch in order to explain to her mother how one of her friends had used a reel to unravel some cocoons into silk. When the mother indicated that she was going to save the drawing among the child's other ones, the girl objected that 'It is not a drawing, but just something to explain how the unravelling was done.' It was not a drawing but a diagram instead, since a drawing is defined by its lack of utility.

3. If, or perhaps more exactly *because*, children regard drawing as a game, they take it very seriously. In general, unless the child has been forced to hurry for some reason, the drawings are carefully executed. On the one hand, the child will often draw them for a specific person or dedicate them to that person in some way; on the other, the child will cast a critical eye over them. We will later consider some of the reasons why children either approve or disapprove of their own drawings. Here it suffices to draw attention to the very fact of this appreciation. Thus a drawing may be deemed 'very pretty' or 'the most beautiful in the whole world'. However, even though children are usually satisfied with their drawings, this is not always the case. Individual differences exist in relation to drawing, as for any other activity: some children are always content, others can be extremely fastidious. Furthermore, the same child may experience periods of satisfaction and then discontentment, without there being any noticeable differences in the quality of the drawings. A young girl from California, almost three years old, accompanied her drawings with the following negative reservations: 'it's a *kind* of sparrow', 'it's a *kind* of cat'. Very often, however, a drawing judged as defective can be a source of amusement rather than of discontent for the child. A four-year-old Belgian boy, having noticed that he had drawn the hair of one of his drawings of people too long, exclaimed: 'This man is funny: he has long hair.' A child, of five-and-a-half, having drawn a horse, burst out laughing: 'Oh! My horse looks like a pig.' Yet another child drew five portraits of his family side by side, and then himself. He was clearly pleased with the other drawings, but laughed at his own portrait: 'What a funny Armand' (his name). A four-year-old German boy made the following

2. See Immanuel Kant (1987/1790), *Critique of judgment* (trans. W.S. Pluhar). New York: Hackett.

comments about his drawing of a man: 'He's an old man; he has no hair at all; the old man is also lame' (in fact, the drawing does not show this).

Often, once they have noticed something wrong, children will come up with an excuse. Sometimes they will appeal to some accidental factor, such as lack of space on the paper, to explain why the arms and legs of a person are too short; sometimes, they resort to rather more sophisticated excuses, with which they probably deceive themselves to some extent. A small boy from California, during the last quarter of his fourth year, was dissatisfied with many of the people he had drawn, but contented himself by calling them Japanese. A three-year-old Belgian girl drew a 'Mummy' limited to just a head. When her attention was drawn to the lack of arms and legs, she replied that 'She has lost her arms, and also her legs.' Another four-year-old drew toes in a portrait of her mother. When she was told that the shoes would not allow the toes to be seen, she said 'Yes, but I have done my mother with bare feet.' When it was pointed out to a five-year-old boy that he had drawn the wheels of a harnessed cart much lower than the feet of the horse, he explained that 'The horse is on a mountain.' At other times, the child simply points out the faults in his drawing without searching for an excuse; he may say, for example, that the drawing or part of it 'was done in a hurry'.

The child's dissatisfaction with a drawing, either when it is finished or during the course of its production, is manifest in various ways. Sometimes children are content to make no comment, carrying on in silence; sometimes they state that 'it is nonsense',

Fig. 1. Simonne Luquet, French, 4;2 (Luquet collection). House. A drawing judged by her to be badly executed and erased (§3).

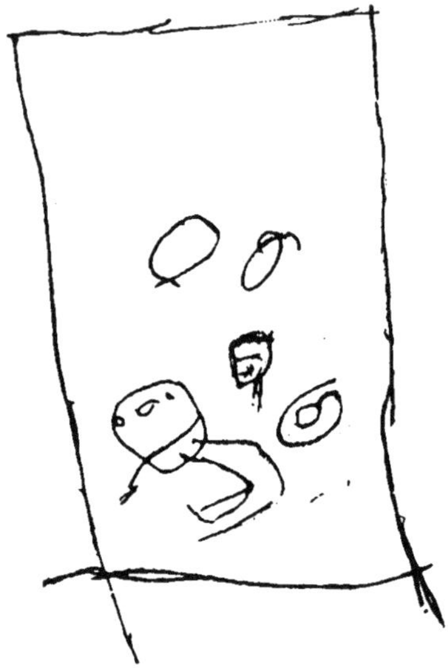

Fig. 2. Simonne Luquet, French, 3;8 (Luquet collection). House.
The drawing begun of a lady in the interior was abandoned and erased (§3).

'nothing at all' or 'it doesn't count'. Sometimes, their dissatisfaction is expressed not in words but actions: the drawing is crumpled up, torn up, or thrown away. Children will also erase them. In the case of ink drawings, they may simply smear them, either by spreading the wet ink with their hand over the paper, or else by turning the paper over and vigorously rubbing it against the table (fig. 1). When just a part of a drawing is judged imperfect, it may be dismissed as a scribble (fig. 2).

4. In various cases, children will correct that part of their drawing judged to be faulty. In some cases, the correction will be explicitly indicated. For example a young girl (4;4)[3] crossed out an arm drawn on the left of a person and drew another arm above the right arm instead. However, by far the most frequent procedure is what I will call 'tacit correction'. Here the child leaves the faulty detail unchanged and simply juxtaposes the corrected version beside it. For example, in a drawing of *Père Janvier*,[4] a young girl (6;7), noticing

3. This should be read as 'aged four years and four months'.
4. At Christmas-time, God-parents give their God-children a cake in the shape of a human figure called *Père Janvier.*

that she had not done the hat properly, drew another one to the right of the first without rubbing it out. The same girl, when drawing a donkey, noticed that the ears were set too far forward on the head, and added two more to the first ones. A five-year-old Belgian girl, who had drawn a woman without clothes, thought about dressing her; she drew a trapezoidal skirt over the primitive legs, which she left as they were, modifying the ends of the legs into two feet. In a drawing by a Belgian boy (5;6) of army conscripts dancing, all the men had their far leg bent, except one where this leg, having been first drawn straight, had then clearly had a bent leg drawn over it.

The reason for this process of correction without erasure is not to be found in a difficulty with the medium since, as we have seen, children do know how to erase things. Thus, if in the majority of cases, they are content to correct their drawing by juxtaposition, instead of substitution, it is clearly because the child simply does not experience any need to physically suppress the defective details. Once the trace is deemed to be faulty, it is as if it no longer exists; the child literally no longer sees it, being hypnotised somehow by the new marks that have replaced it, and no longer notices the lines which accidentally occurred on the paper. This is a manifestation of a spontaneous faculty for selection or abstraction that is also responsible for the fact that children do not bother to reproduce all of the actual features of an object in their drawings. It is as if they do not see any of the features that do not interest them.

Fig. 3. Simonne Luquet, French, 5;6 (Luquet collection). *Père Janvier*. Intention suggested by external circumstances (§8). The hat is corrected by a tacit correction (§4). The sack is displaced by intellectual realism (§77).

Fig. 4. Simonne Luquet, French, 6;4 (Luquet collection). Toy (spinning top). Intention determined by graphic homonymy (§11).

5. Drawing or graphic activity is composed of two elements: the activity of drawing in general and the execution of a specific drawing. What are the motifs or subjects treated by children in their spontaneous drawings? Everyone knows that the human figure is by far the most frequent. But the repertoire is not limited to this, and often added to such pictures are 'gee-gees', 'ladies', and houses. My own examination of a complete collection of one child's drawings revealed every possible category of creatures and objects, and also all kinds of genres adopted by professional artists: portraits, landscapes, still lives, drawings based on legendary or historical events (which children treat as identical), genre painting, and illustrations of real or imagined stories.

Certainly, the body of work drawn even by the same artist can, depending on the particular child, show striking differences both in the overall number of drawings and in the nature and relative proportion of the different motifs. Many different children show a marked and sometimes exclusive predilection to reproduce a certain category of objects. Such specialisation can become a vocation and reflects something about the child's individual character. A most curious example of this comes from a well-known archaeologist who, when he was no more than four, had a veritable passion for umbrellas which neither he nor his parents could explain. He would never go out without an umbrella, drew them continually, and would often ask the grown-ups around him to draw them for him.

Nevertheless, even when taking into account these idiosyncrasies, one can formulate a general rule that children represent everything in their drawings that forms part of their experience, everything that presents itself in their perception. Even the differences in their interest in this or that category of objects are determined not only by their personal taste, but also by the conditions of their existence, and the way their interests vary with those conditions. Thus young 'animal painters' (*animaliers*) live in the country or in a family home in constant contact with domestic animals, such as dogs, birds, and horses. The graphic repertoire of the child, along with his or her visual experience, is determined by the surroundings in which he or she lives. A study in the public schools in Berlin, to determine which objects would be likely to be drawn, found that children over six years had never seen the following objects: rivers, 98 per cent, birch trees, 87 per cent, live hares, 75 per cent, squirrels, 64 per cent, fields of grain, 59 per cent, snails, 53 per cent. In Boston, children between four and eight had never seen the following: crows , 77 per cent, blackberries, 66 per cent, ducks, 65 per cent, fields of potatoes, 61 per cent, sparrows, 57 per cent, frogs, 50 per cent, and butterflies, 20 per cent.

6. In their earliest drawings, children, though they know and are also able to represent many objects, nevertheless choose to depict only a single object in any particular drawing. It is not possible to determine the largely unconscious motives and reasons that lead the child to draw just that particular object. But it is possible to formulate the following general principle: the drawings are, in essence, graphic gestures, provoked like any other gesture by the intimate connection between the physical and mental. The intention to draw a certain object is the extension and manifestation of the child's mental representation: the object depicted is that which, in the mind of the artist, has momentarily come to take an exclusive or preponderant position. The factors that lead the child to draw any particular object are tied up with those that give rise to the ideas of the corresponding object.

7. Primary among these factors is the influence of the external circumstances. Among these, we should set to one side any instructions the child may receive from someone else to produce a certain drawing. These external suggestions have only a very limited and fleeting influence, and they do not seem to be as effective as those motifs that the child is already drawing spontaneously. Thus a girl a little over three-and-a-half showed her grandmother a drawing of balloons she had just finished, which conformed to her habitual type, consisting of a round shape covered with rectangular marks. Her grandmother asked if they were griddle cakes. Although this could have been taken as a suggestion to draw griddle cakes, especially given that the child had already drawn some cakes, she never subsequently drew any griddle cakes.

8. Unlike suggestions in the strict sense (i.e. instructions from other people), external circumstances do not impose their 'will' on the child, even though they may somehow influence his or her spontaneity. They propose rather than impose a motif to the child. They are involved in all drawings suggested by the perception or memory of the corresponding objects. These objects can be of two kinds: either actual objects or else models, that is, either drawings already produced earlier by the same child, or pictures created by other people and found in albums, books or catalogues.

I could cite a host of drawings whose intention was determined by the perception of real objects or by the immediate surroundings.

Thus, in the case of one child, five drawings of horses were provoked, as she herself explained, by the sight of a horse going along the street; a drawing of a postage stamp after having looked at a stamp album; and that of a man producing soap bubbles after she had complained she had nothing to do and her brother had suggested she might blow some soap bubbles. The drawing of a walk in the snow was drawn on 20 December (fig. 62). The drawings of children of various nationalities reproduce events which they have had read to them from the newspaper, such as a wedding, attempted murder, shipwreck, or lightning striking a house (fig. 138).

Other drawings are inspired by less immediate circumstances but those still occurring on the same day, such as incidents relating to a walk taken by the child, a button the child has found and brought back home, a circus or concert to which she had been taken, the mouse which had been caught in the mouse trap, the stove that was lit again at the beginning of winter.

The drawings can also be determined by much earlier events, thanks to the ability, which is especially marked in childhood, to revive the most distant memories. For example, one girl in her drawing of a garden depicted 'mignonette seeds about to grow' even though these had been planted eight months earlier. The two legendary heroes of Douai, Gayant and his wife, were drawn with great accuracy and detail even though they were drawn from memory after a six-day delay (their accuracy can easily be confirmed by comparing the drawings with the corresponding photograph; see figs 37–45). The last of the drawings of Gayant is the most complete; it reproduces the helmet with its crest of feathers, the flowing cape, the coat of mail and the armour for the thighs, the lance and the shield decorated in its centre with the gothic 'd' which served as the arms for the town of Douai. The drawing of Madame Gayant shows her earrings, the rings on her fingers, the fan and the chain of gems hanging across her breast. Another drawing accurately reproduces in incredible detail the area of a town where this child spent her holidays and which she had not seen for five months.

Quite often, the memories that suggest drawings to the child are provoked by the closeness and expectation of the return of similar circumstances. Thus, with the approach of the holidays, the child may draw the country, or scenes or objects that had been seen on previous holidays, for example the seaside.

Finally, the drawings sometimes relate to ideas suggested by more prolonged events. In the case of many children, one finds at the end of December repeated drawings of Saint Nicholas or *Père Janvier* (fig. 3), of 'dolls like the ones in the shop windows', and Christmas trees. At the beginning of the [First World] War, the graffiti in the streets in France frequently showed soldiers with pointed helmets, a motif which would not have been encountered before; and anyone can confirm that every year on the 1st of April there is a veritable outburst of drawings of fish on the walls in the most diverse localities.[5]

9. I could go on and on giving examples of how models can determine the child's intention to draw. For a great many children, their first drawings pretend to reproduce the same motifs as drawings produced by their parents, often those requested by the children themselves. At later ages, one can find numerous drawings by many different children that have been suggested by drawings that had been produced in their presence by brothers and sisters or their young friends. One young girl's only drawings of cats up to the age of four were cats seen from behind, which she subsequently distinguished from cats in profile by the name of sitting cats; these were inspired by the picture of a cat represented from behind which decorated the ashtray on her father's table which she could see while she was drawing.

As we have seen, the intention can be provoked either by the perception or by the memory of real objects or by drawn models. However, only in a limited number of special cases is it possible to definitely determine whether one or other of these factors has been involved. In any case, it seems arbitrary to give to any one of these elements a predominant role.

According to a wide range of authors, children do not draw, at least at the outset, from the objects actually present before them; that is to say, even when the intention to draw is provoked by real objects, it is through their memory rather than perception of them. This opinion does not correspond with the facts, and I could readily cite many examples where children have explicitly declared that they are going to reproduce an object in front of their eyes. Sometimes it is even the case that when they wish to find a subject for their drawing they will seek out objects which are available for them to see. Thus the claim is false in terms of the evidence. And the theoretical argument to support it is no better. The child, it is

5. On the 1st of April cut-out paper fish are stuck on other people's backs as a prank to fool them.

claimed, would not experience any need to have an image of an object when it has the object itself: 'any more than does a lover feel the need to make a portrait of his mistress while she is beside him'. This argument is based on a radical misunderstanding of the role that children give to their drawings. The drawing is in no way a substitute for the corresponding object, of inferior value and redundant in the presence of the object itself. It is the work *(l'oeuvre)* of the child, the product and manifestation of her creative activity, and the operation of this faculty and the accompanying pleasure remain the same whether or not the drawing represents an object that is present or absent.

It has also been maintained that the child is more inspired by models drawn by other people than by actual objects. I readily admit that at the very beginning, when children have not yet developed a graphic repertoire, other people's drawings provide them with already familiar themes that direct their intention towards drawing something. It is even possible that, by virtue of the joy children get from becoming conscious of their faculty for graphic creation (which we regard as fundamental to the aesthetics of children; see §58), they might more or less unconsciously try to prove themselves equal to adults by producing just the same drawings they have seen them make.

Yet this is not how the role of models is usually understood: children are supposed to imitate them not because they provide ideas for drawings, but because they make their own drawings easier to produce. The representation of real objects, it is claimed, presents the beginning artist with the difficulty of translating three dimensions onto a two-dimensional surface, whereas the child is supposed to avoid this difficulty by copying drawings where this translation has already been done for him.

Later, I will set out a general criticism of the idea that children are supposed to be guided more or less unconsciously in their choice of subjects by their relative ease of execution (§38). Here I will simply note that in those drawings with the express purpose of copying a model, the model merely provides the subject of the drawing. What inspires children is not the actual object in front of them (for most of the time it is not even looked at) but what I will call 'the internal model' (§35). The child is no more concerned with perspective when copying drawings or drawing from nature than when drawing from memory. In place of perspective, the child substitutes another mode of representation, a changing point of view. It is therefore entirely wrong to attribute to children an adult conception quite alien to their mentality, namely, the use of other people's drawings as models in the strict sense of the word: that is, not just as a source of inspiration, but as an example from which to copy how adults represent real objects, thereby making the child's own drawing easier to produce.

10. A second factor influencing the intention is the association of ideas. The overall appearance of a drawing is accompanied by the more or less conscious idea of the corresponding object: this evokes by association the idea of a different object which then becomes the new intention for the artist. For a multitude of children from many different countries, the first drawings of a woman or mummy immediately suggest a drawing of a man or daddy. The first horse drawn by one girl came alongside that of a whip, and the passage from one to the other is demonstrated by the comments of this child: 'This is a whip; it is necessary for riding the horse.' A drawing of a postage stamp provokes that of an envelope. Various drawings of trains are followed immediately by drawings of cars; conversely, a car follows a train or else a horse rider (figs 8 and 9). The association of ideas is also apparent in consecutive drawings of bread, a plate, a bottle, and of a knife, fork, and spoon. An American girl wanted to represent the story of John Nose-in-the-Air[6] and began to draw John having fallen into the water and two men on the shore coming to pull him out. But these men at the edge of the water suggested the idea of fishing, and she put a fishing rod in their hands with a fish suspended from them. The caught fish in turn evoked the idea of fish, and the rest of the sheet of paper was filled by drawings of fish.

11. Special note should be made of a special case of association by resemblance, where the analogy is no longer intellectual (based on function) but visual (analogy by appearance). For this reason, I will refer to such cases as analogies based on shape. This process of analogy occurs in two distinct forms: objective and graphic morphological analogy (which could also be called graphic ambiguity); in the first case, the resemblance is based on the *appearance* of the objects depicted, in the second on similarities between their *representations* in the drawing. It is often impossible to differentiate the

6. See E. Barnes (1893). A study on children's drawings. *Pedagogical Seminary, 2(3)*, 455–63. This study was based on a mere 6393 drawings of John Nose-in-the-Air.

Fig. 5. Simonne Luquet, French, 3;5 (Luquet collection). Horse. The intention was determined by association of ideas (§10).

Fig. 6. Simonne Luquet, French, 6;8 (Luquet collection). Hen. Interpretation suggested by the appearance of the lines (§16).

two, the resemblance of the drawings simply arising from the resemblance of the corresponding objects, as in the case of drawings of a man and a woman. But in certain cases, especially in the earliest drawings, the child's lack of skill gives rise to a resemblance which does not exist between the actual objects, and thus one can tell it is a case of analogy based on the form of the drawing. Hence, although there is little resemblance between the shapes of an actual steeple, man, fish and cat, the drawings of these different motifs by a girl of about four-and-a-half were each formed by an ellipse and, over a variety of repeated drawings, each one suggested the next (figs 10 and 11). The influence of analogy based on shape or form is especially clear in the following example. Over several days, the same girl, at 6;4, drew numbers, especially eights. Beside one of these, she drew a spinning top which has roughly the same form, and then completed this drawing with sticks connected by string (fig. 4). For a boy of 4;1 the drawing of a pipe suggested that of an ankle boot through the effect of graphic homology.

12. A third factor influencing the intention, which I will term graphic automatism, is similar to the association of ideas in that a drawing is provoked by one drawn earlier. But in this case, the two drawings represent the same object. Nothing intervenes between the representation corresponding to the first drawing and that which

Figs 7–9. Simonne Luquet, French, 7;6 (Luquet collection). Three consecutive drawings.

Fig. 7. Lady carrying an umbrella. The addition of a detail was provoked by external circumstances (§31).

Fig. 8. Horse rider. Addition of a detail was provoked by external circumstances (§31).

Fig. 9. Horse and carriage. The intention was suggested by association of ideas (§10). Note the rabattement of the wheels (§76).

suggests the unconscious intention that becomes realised in the subsequent drawings. The original 'evocative' drawing is mechanically reproduced in a series of examples. A first case of graphic automatism is that of immediate graphic automatism where one drawing is immediately followed by yet another or several other drawings of the same subject. Among a host of such examples, I will here borrow some from a Belgian writer. A child of three-and-a-half drew for half an hour a considerable number of small crooked lines in the rough form of an 'm' or a 'w'. A girl of the same age covered both sides of her slate and then a sheet of paper with small round shapes. Another girl, also three-and-a-half, drew a line of more than a hundred 'men' each composed of a circle and two lines. The next day, when invited to draw, she returned to the same stereotype, but did so more slowly and added two eyes to the head: in half an hour she drew more than a hundred of these 'tadpole men'.[7] A Californian

7. *Homme sans tronc* or *bonhomme têtard*. In these drawings, a person is depicted simply by a circular form (with facial features) to which arms and legs are attached.

boy of 3;8 drew a line of 40 'photographs of myself when I was a baby'. An American child, having set out to draw a representation of the story of John Nose-in-the-Air forgot his intention and lined up 26 figures of John.

13. In addition to immediate graphic automatism (where the same drawing is repeated in rapid succession), there is also continuous graphic automatism, the automatic tendency to repeat the same drawing over the course of one or several days, in the absence of any observable mental causes. We have already considered an example of immediate automatism in relation to the drawings of men produced by a Belgian girl. Another child, who drew a long series of circles as a result of immediate automatism, a little later on drew nothing but ladders for more than eight days, each consisting of two horizontal lines cut by several vertical lines (there were almost always five of these). Over a period of two days, a five-year-old incessantly drew men without any trunk and with their arms fixed to their legs. For several days, a five-year-old Belgian boy drew tables to the exclusion of any other subject, regardless of what his teacher requested; these tables were drawn according to a schema he had learnt in a lesson about sticks (*bâtonnets*): a rectangle with two of its short sides extended so as to form legs; and with a dot inside the rectangle to represent the handle of the drawer (fig. 11). In the case of a French girl (4;3), this automatism had an almost obsessive quality relating to the subject of houses. Over the course of 14 days, the 16 drawings she produced were solely of houses; 6 days later she began again with a series which lasted for 18 days and consisted of 31 houses and nothing else: 3 months later, having only drawn different motifs, she commented: 'It's been a long time since I drew any houses' and then drew one.

14. The intention is not only influenced by one or other of the factors already discussed, but also by their joint action. For example, after drawing a series of cats (fig.10), a child produced a drawing that she described as a steeple (fig. 11). An intention to draw yet more cats might have been expected through graphic automatism. However, because the shape of the cat drawings suggested a steeple, this intention became transformed into a different intention to draw a steeple instead. In fact, the latter was the only intention she announced. Nevertheless, the intention to draw a cat evidently survived unconsciously despite her declared intention to draw a steeple. For although the drawing was claimed to be a steeple, it retained the horizontal line she used to attach to the end of her cat

drawings to represent the tail, even though there was no reason, of course, for it to appear on a steeple. Of course, as a psychological

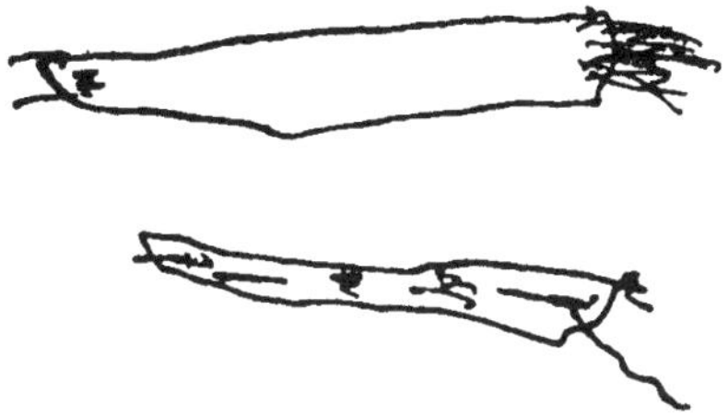

Figs 10 and 11. Simonne Luquet, French, 4;2 (Luquet collection). Immediately consecutive drawings of a cat and then a steeple. The intention of the latter was determined by a graphic homonymy (§11).

explanation the association of ideas is extremely vague, since it can always justify the elicitation of one idea by another. An explanation of why any particular idea is provoked at any given time requires an appeal to additional factors. In relation to the present topic, the external circumstances can (as has been noted) have a direct effect on the intention to draw, but they can also have an indirect effect by directing the association of ideas in one direction or another. Thus a girl (4;6) drew five men and women side by side on the same sheet of paper, but since it was just after Christmas, these figures evoked the idea of people making visits, and so she went on to draw the roads along which they had come. Similarly, one day the drawing of a fish provoked the memory of fishing (angling) parties which she had taken part in during her holidays, and so she added to the fish a fishing scene. But some days later, another drawing of fish made her think of two live fish which were being kept at home in a bowl, and this drawing was immediately followed by two others, each representing a bowl with two fish. A drawing of a marguerite at first suggested two roses and some violets, and then, since it was All Saints' Day (when people take wreaths of flowers to the cemeteries) a wreath of flowers.

2
The Interpretation

15. Either while creating the drawing or once it is finished, the child will give it some interpretation. The intention is the perpetuation of the idea the child had in mind when starting to do the drawing, whereas, the interpretation arises from an idea that occurs to the child during the course of doing the drawing and to which he or she applies a name.

Usually, the latter idea is the same as that which, in the form of an intention, suggested the drawing in the first place, and indeed the very act of producing the drawing helps to keep it in mind. But this is not always the case. Observation has revealed the neglected fact that the child will often give to the finished drawing an interpretation that differs from the original intention. It is possible to list a limitless number of such examples taken from the most diverse children. In the case of one girl, who was almost four, a frog became a dog, another became a person; conversely a drawing that was declared to be of a person was deemed, once finished, to be a frog. A drawing by a girl (4;6) provides an interesting example of an extreme difference between the intention and the interpretation (fig. 12). When she had finished it, she interpreted it as a sheep, and when asked to identify the parts she pointed out the head, eye, mouth, legs, and wool. She was completely satisfied with this drawing. She exclaimed that the head was just like that of a sheep, and indeed the next day, thinking again about this drawing in relation to another sheep she wanted to draw, she repeated: 'It had just the right shape for a sheep.' From the satisfaction this drawing gave her, one might suppose that it corresponded to her original intention, yet that had been completely different. Seeing her mother tracing embroidery designs, she wanted to do the same thing and traced one of the designs. Her copy had accidentally taken the form that she interpreted as a sheep, and hence she completed it according to the interpretation she had now added. More remarkable still are cases where a 'blot' of ink, though completely accidental, is taken by different children to be one of their intended drawings and is then given some interpretation, such as a dog, or an ocean.

Fig. 12. Simonne Luquet, French, 4;6 (Luquet collection). Sheep. The interpretation differed from the intention (§15). The illusion that she knew how to draw the motif determined the intention (§21).

Fig. 13. Simonne Luquet, French, 3;11 (Luquet collection). Cushion. The interpretation differed from the intention (§18).

What is the source of the interpretation, whether it is the same as the original intention, or (as sometimes happens) different? As we shall shortly see (§17), the interpretation is most often determined by the resemblance between the drawing and an object familiar to the child, and since the name of this object is used in the interpretation of the drawing I call it the designated object. The force with which the interpretation strikes the child depends on how much resemblance there is between the drawing and the designated object, or, to be more precise, the child's internal model of that object (§34). Now this resemblance is highly variable because, even for the same child, the different subjects or motifs are not the same 'age', as it were. If, for example, the child is drawing a line of men and dogs, it could be that this is the first time she has drawn a dog but the fiftieth time for the man, with the inevitable consequence that the man will be drawn with greater graphic skill. Furthermore, with practice, the child acquires not only the skill to draw a certain motif, but also the general skill of drawing, which is to say creating a correspondence between the actions of drawing and the representation of any object. Thus, the first cat drawing might be considerably less imperfect than the first dog, if it is produced three months later, because the child's general graphic skill would have improved through the overall effect of any drawings created in that interval.

The extent to which the interpretation and the intention coincide will vary according to how much the drawing corresponds to the child's original intention, and hence this lack of coincidence will largely be a function of the child's skill in drawing. This explains the observed fact that cases of non-coincidence gradually diminish with skill acquired though practice in drawing.

16. The positive and rather substantial force supporting the interpretation derives from the resemblance between the drawing and the designated object. But this positive force is counteracted by a negative one, since the interpretation does not occur in isolation but has to be reconciled with the intention the child originally had in mind. The intention, like any other mental state, tends to persist in immediate memory, and this memory of the intention has, as does the interpretation, a rather substantial intrinsic power. The power of the interpretation depends upon the resemblance between the drawing and its designated object; that of the intention depends on the resemblance between the drawing and the object that suggested it, and, above all, with the child's internal model of that object, which is nothing other than the representative aspect of that intention.

The memory of the intention, which persists rather powerfully in the child's consciousness, clashes with the interpretation that begins to emerge under the influence of the drawing itself. When, as a result of lack of skill in drawing, the germ of the interpretation differs from the intention, their coming together in consciousness gives rise to a conflict. Here, as elsewhere in mental life, this conflict between mental elements involves a struggle to arrive at a resolution through their reciprocal effects. On the one hand, the intention strives to persist and set itself up in opposition to the emerging interpretation and prevent it from developing; on the other hand, the emerging interpretation struggles to substitute its own development in place of the memory of the opposing intention. Clearly, the outcome of this conflict will depend on the relative power of the two adversaries, and their power derives solely from the extent to which they each accord with the drawing itself, that is, the resemblance of the drawing to the object that suggested the intention, and with the object designated in the interpretation.

I should add, however, that the intrinsic force of the intention can, independently of any conflict with a different interpretation, be reduced to some extent or even eliminated by another purely mental factor. This factor is the child's labile mental condition,[8] a

8. *'mobilité'*.

characteristic trait that is universally recognised by child psychologists. If children have an extraordinary memory for events which happened long ago and recall them with almost perfect clarity (§8), in another sense they are essentially forgetful: they live in the here-and-now without attempting to reconcile it with even immediately preceding events. This is the reason why children add details to some of their drawings that are incompatible with the rest of the drawing (§32), since whilst producing the drawing they have forgotten the original intention. Thus one can see how, because of this fickleness of mind, children may come to forget their intention either while in the act of drawing or even before they have begun. I have already noted examples of this. In these circumstances, an intrinsically weak interpretation with very little resemblance to the designated object can readily replace the intention, simply because the latter had disappeared from the child's consciousness.

Depending upon their intensities, the conflict between the intention and the interpretation can have a variety of outcomes. When the memory of the intention is intrinsically strong and the interpretation weak, children generally limit themselves to admitting that the drawing has not worked with such comments as 'it isn't anything at all'. When both the intention and the interpretation are inherently weak, the result is that the interpretation itself is feeble. This is manifested in various ways. The child may abandon his interpretation if it is challenged, may only announce it after some hesitation, or else may give several different interpretations in quick succession or else none at all.

When the memory of the intention and the interpretation are both inherently strong, they coexist and compete with one another in the mind of the child. Children are aware of this conflict in their very first drawings. At first, the way they express this conflict is unclear; the child says, for example, 'it is a fish; it isn't a fish', which no doubt can be translated as 'I am interpreting my drawing as a fish because it looks like one, not because I meant to draw one.' But later, they put it more precisely and refer to the mental process of substituting an interpretation that is different from the original intention. Among many examples from many different children, I will refer to a drawing by a girl just a little over six-and-a-half (fig. 6) where she spontaneously noted 'I didn't mean to draw a hen, but I can see that it looks like a hen.'

When the memory of the intention is inherently weak and the interpretation inherently strong, the outcome is straightforward, and the child maintains her interpretation regardless, whether or not it is really justifiable. In particular, if someone points out some detail in the drawing which conflicts with the interpretation, or if the child notices it herself, she will contrive to give this detail an interpretation which allows it to conform to the rest of the drawing.

In most cases, the justifications given by children for such irreconcilable details, like other imperfections in their drawings, are naive rather than contrived. As strange as it may seem, children sometimes forget not only what it is they meant to draw, but even that the drawings are their own work. Taken in by their own imagination, they genuinely mistake their drawings for real objects in the same way that they take sometimes shapeless representations or images for their own graphic creations. Thus a four-year-old French girl, having drawn a man with a cigarette in his mouth, put the top back on her pen and brought its tip towards the end of the cigarette as if to light it. It was only after this little show that she drew smoke around the cigarette. A German girl (4;6) drew a picture of the holy family. She first drew the infant Jesus, but did not show him praying: the knees were not bent and instead of hands being held together one could see a tangled mass. The girl was indignant with this: 'Naughty Jesus doesn't want to pray, and Joseph is very angry and stamps and shouts because he won't kneel and pray. Naughty Jesus, you really ought to kneel down and pray!' At the same time, she drew Joseph with his leg in the air: in his anger he is stamping on the ground. Finally, she managed to draw a kneeling figure with its hands together; the child had come to behave itself. This seemingly sophisticated mechanism of justification is especially clear in a drawing by a girl (5;4) in which a young girl had her face covered by a black blot. Pointing this out to the girl, I asked her 'Is this a beard?' She replied very reasonably 'Of course not, since it is a small girl. It's because my pen had too much ink.' She knew full well that this detail was just the result of an accident. But, although this blot had no significance in the drawing she meant to make, it was necessary to give it one now it existed, and so she added: 'She has thrown up (*rendu*) all her wine over her mouth.' This justification may seem to us rather sophisticated, but it is certainly not for the child: it is simply an interpretation of the drawing regarded as an object in its own right, independently of the intention that led her to draw it. A small boy (5;8) who had drawn a woman with extremely large feathers in her hat, interpreted it as 'a woman with a Christmas tree which has sprouted on her head', and he was so pleased with this interpretation that he drew beside it 'a gentleman (her husband) with a Christmas tree growing out his head'.

17. According to the preceding discussion, it follows that the interpretations children give their drawings, either while they are drawing them or when they are finished, can differ from the intention which originally gave rise to them. The child cannot explain the drawing by the original intention and seeks for one, instead, in the resulting drawing.

But the influence of the drawing in determining the interpretation that the child imposes upon it, when the interpretation and the original interpretation differ, can occur in various ways. In other words, the actual structure of the drawing can support the interpretation in different ways. With the exception of graphic automatism, which in its very essence influences the intention but not the interpretation, the factors that affect the interpretation are the same as those influencing the intention.

Among these factors, one which occurs either alone or in combination in almost all cases is analogy of shape, the resemblance between the drawing and the designated object (or more precisely the internal model of that object), or, in other words, the object whose name has been given to the drawing. This resemblance most often occurs at the global level, between the overall appearance of the drawing and the designated object (which itself could be a motif or real object, or else a model or a drawing).

Sometimes children introduce details that are incompatible with the rest of the drawing (§32). When what is depicted in the drawing is completely unambiguous, these incompatible details are regarded by the child simply as superimposed, and no attention is paid to

Fig. 14. Simonne Luquet, French, 7;8 (Luquet collection). Train. Transformation of the lantern of the train into a head through analogy in shape (§17 et seq.). The wheels do not show rabattement (§76) and are depicted whole (§73).

them. Any new interpretation of the entire drawing which had either provoked these additions or else been provoked by them dissipates before entering the child's consciousness. This is the case for the buttons drawn on the body of a cat which was given a kind of coat, and for the details which transformed the lantern of a steam train into a human face (fig. 14). If the attention of the child is drawn to these details, she disowns them or else tries to offer a new and rather sophisticated account of the entire drawing (§32). This only happens if the entire drawing is sufficiently vague that it is susceptible to an interpretation that can give some sense to those details. This would explain the extreme rarity of cases where the interpretation of a drawing is determined, not by its resemblance to the designated object, but by a partial resemblance. To be honest, I have encountered no absolutely definitive examples of this. The determining influence of a detail on the interpretation can only be recognised with any certainty for drawings that combine two incompatible details. Thus a girl (4;6) having drawn a man who had both a pipe and earrings, interpreted it as a woman. When the pipe was pointed out, she declared that it was the husband of the woman she had just drawn. On showing her the earrings, she said 'Those are earrings, this woman here has earrings': she thus returned to the interpretation that it was a woman. But when she was again shown the pipe, she reverted to her interpretation of the drawing as a man, and, in order to dismiss the details which could only be taken for earrings, she chose to see them as simple ornamental details devoid of any representational significance: 'They aren't earrings; I did them to make the drawing pretty; in any case, he's smoking a pipe.'

In combination with the dominant role of analogies based on shape in determining the interpretation, there is the inevitable fact that the influence of resemblance on the interpretation is much greater when it is applied after the event than when it merely continues the original intention. If one compares two drawings by

Figs 15 and 16. Simonne Luquet, French, 3;6 (Luquet collection). Drawing interpreted after it was drawn as a hand, followed by one which was intended to be a hand (§17).

a young girl (3;5), which were drawn immediately after one another, the second drawing was meant to be a hand, whereas the first was only given this interpretation after it had been finished (figs 15 and 16). This is easily explained. In the case of a premeditated drawing, the memory of the intention is enough to sustain it, even if the drawing bears little resemblance to it. In this case, imposing an interpretation is restricted to repeating the intention, even if the child happens to find no resemblance between the drawing and the object being drawn, or thinks the drawing is unsuccessful, or even if an alternative interpretation would conform better to how the drawing turned out. But when the interpretation differs from the intention, the child needs to find some justification for this in the resemblance between the drawing and the designated object.

18. If, in general, the interpretation of a drawing can be linked to an analogy in shape between the drawing and the designated object, this explanation remains insufficient in those cases where an analogy based on shape would provide as good, or even better, justifications for a host of alternative interpretations. According to our general scheme, the interpretation attaches a name to the drawing corresponding to the idea the child had in mind when producing the drawing. Usually, this idea is suggested by the drawing itself through analogy of shape, whether or not it is different from the original intention. But it can also be provoked by the same factors which influence the original intention and more generally the elicitation of any idea, namely, external circumstances and the association of ideas. For example, a girl's drawing (3;4) closely resembled an immediately preceding one she had claimed to be a person, and presumably the new one was intended to be the same. The fact that she interpreted the second drawing, however, as a fish seems most likely explained by the fact that at that moment she was amused by some live fish in a bowl of water. Similarly, a month later, she produced a drawing which strongly resembled one she had drawn the day before and had interpreted as a parrot. The fact that the later drawing was interpreted as a cat is most likely owing to association of ideas since this drawing had immediately followed one of a mouse.

But reality puts limits on our grand formulas, and I should point out a factor which in some cases determines the interpretation, one which bears some analogy to the kind of deception sometimes engaged in by participants in research in experimental psychology. This involves a kind of teasing which causes the child to give an interpretation different from what the observer would expect. Thus, at almost four years, my daughter, having announced that she would draw a house, then drew a square (fig. 13), which was just like the shape of houses from the front or back. She then showed it to me, saying: 'You don't know what this is. – Yes. – No. It's a house. – No: it's a cushion; (and as proof) here is the bow' (that is, the connection of the cord which serves as the hem). When her mother turned up, she showed her the drawing and gave the same interpretation. As I see it, such teasing is only incidental to the fundamental mental process. The girl meant to draw a house and had finished the drawing, but this then suggested through analogy of shape the interpretation of cushion (in fact, there was a cushion in the house which she found particularly interesting). This gave rise to a conflict in her mind between the original intention and the final interpretation, and she transferred this conflict to me by claiming it was a cushion rather than a house.

There are some examples very close to this that one could call graphic puns involving a combination of different elements that can give the entire drawing different possible meanings. Children are probably not often able to invent these themselves, but they take great pleasure in reproducing them once they have been shown them. For example, there are '6–4–2 portraits' in which a profile of the human face is made up of a chain of numbers: 6 for the forehead and the eye, 4 for the nose, 2 for the mouth and the chin. Such drawings are reproduced all over walls, in a wide range of places, by children who have learnt it at school. On a pavement in Paris, near to an advertisement for stove cleaner representing a person whose body and limbs were made out of stove pipes, a child had carefully copied the essence of this image. Then, fascinated by this, he went on to develop the idea creatively in two contiguous attempts by representing a young girl in the form of a coffee grinder, giving it the caption 'Yvonne is a coffee grinder.'

19. It is not just the entire drawing that can be given an interpretation differing from the original intention, but one or more of the details. The interpretation of such details is caused by the same factors as that of the entire drawing. Here is how the childish labile mind and imagination manifested themselves in a drawing by a young girl (5;4) who used a scribble to represent a bedroom. As in her previous drawings, the bedside table, like that of her parents, showed a box of pills and a lamp on it. But once drawn, this became 'a glass of steaming lime tea' which she explained by saying 'the man is ill'.

In a drawing of a house (fig. 17), a detail originally meant to be a gutter with a drainage pipe became interpreted, through analogy of shape, as an umbrella instead. The influence of external circumstances is demonstrated by a table drawn by a young girl in several of her pictures of houses; this initially corresponded to a table for eating outside but was interpreted in a later drawing as a card-table because she had seen her father playing cards with his friends on the table in his office.

Figure 17. Simonne Luquet, French, 4;9 (Luquet collection). House. Change of interpretation of a detail through analogy of shape. Chimney in the air (§68). Indented roof (§69).

Fig. 18. English, 6 years (after Sully). Man. Multiplication of fingers (§32).

At other times, it is because of its relation to the rest of the drawing that a detail comes to receive an interpretation different from its original meaning. For example, in a drawing of a dog by a young girl (3;6), a short line was used to connect two of the main contours that had failed to meet. When she was asked what the line was, she replied 'It's the tail.' At 4;3 she noticed that she had inadvertently drawn the hair of a man at the bottom of his head and his feet in the air. Then, in order to explain these details, she identified as the two eyes, not the lines which were originally intended to be the eyes, but two lines which were supposed to be the beard. It can also happen that a line produced in relation to one drawing may be treated as a detail of another nearby drawing on the same sheet of paper. Thus a drawing announced as a steeple became the yard of the house beside which it had been drawn (figs 19 and 20).

The interpretation of a detail can depend on the meaning given to the drawing which it forms or of which it seems to form a part, and it is natural for it to be modified to correspond to a new

Figs 19 and 20. Simonne Luquet, French, 4;6 (Luquet collection). A house. The part to the right, drawn independently as a steeple, was, after its completion, interpreted as the yard of the house and was then given details corresponding to this interpretation (§19).

interpretation. For example, a drawing meant to represent a small vase in the form of a frog was afterwards interpreted as a person and then completed with the appropriate details (fig. 21): the ellipse on the side, explicitly referred to as the handle of the vase, became a lamp carried by the person. A drawing deemed to be of a house eventually became a clock tower, no doubt because of its elongated shape, and the chimney of the house then became the weather vane on top of the tower, despite the smoke coming out of it.

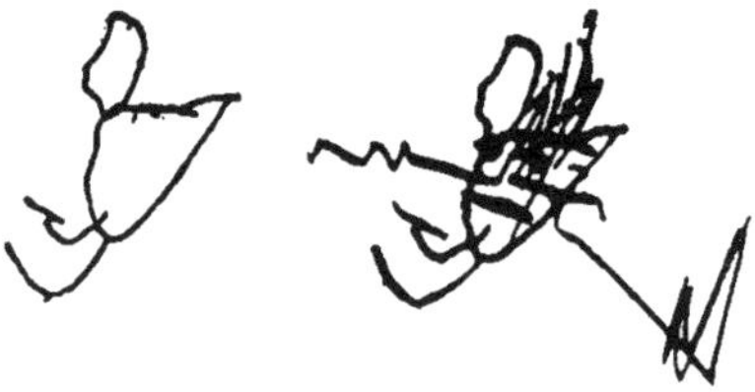

Fig. 21. Simonne Luquet, French, 3;6 (Luquet collection). Two successive states of the same drawing, initially interpreted as a frog, then as a man, which led to a changed interpretation of a detail which had already been drawn (§19), and the addition of new details (§20).

The factors that give rise to the original *intention* can lead the child to add details incompatible with the overall intention of the drawing (§32). Similarly, the factors that influence the *interpretation* can lead the child, after having drawn a detail consistent with the overall interpretation of the drawing, to give it an interpretation incompatible with the overall drawing. This is the case, for example, for the interpretation of an umbrella given, through analogy of shape, to the detail of the house corresponding to the gutter and down pipe (fig. 17).

20. Once, for whatever reason, a drawing has been given an interpretation differerent from the original intention, this interpretation becomes a kind of secondary intention which often provokes the addition of appropriate details to the drawing. Thus a four-year-old Belgian boy, having drawn a fish, interpreted it as a mouse and then added a long tail. In the example we have just discussed of the French girl (3;6) who came to interpret her drawing of a frog as a man, she then added eyes, hair, arms, and a mouth with a pipe (fig. 21). In a drawing she did a year later, where she interpreted a drawing begun as a steeple as a courtyard (fig. 20), she completed it with appropriate details, which she announced as she was drawing them: a flower bed (a kind of scribble against the side of the house), and pots of flowers shaped like dumb bells, where she explicitly distinguished the flower, the stem, and the pot. A French boy (5;10) wanted to draw an 'A' but the form his drawing came to take suggested to him the idea of 'a small rabbit', and he completed his drawing accordingly by adding the hindquarters, the eye, and the paws.

21. The preceding discussion allows us to understand how, through a gradual process of enrichment, the graphic repertoire of the child comes to include the whole range of different subjects that we in fact observe. If graphic automatism forces the child to repeat the same motifs, the effect of external circumstances and the association of ideas gives rise to the intention to produce new drawings. Often, the idea corresponding to an already completed drawing evokes through association the idea of another object which has never been drawn and which thus becomes a new motif. For example, the first drawing of a daddy can be provoked by a drawing of mummy, or a drawing of a mouse by that of a cat. Often it can also happen that the drawing of one object suggests, by means of association by contiguity, a second object which is then drawn beside it, and the two together come to form a new motif. The resulting complex motif, retained in the memory of the child, can

become the starting point for a series of analogous drawings. For example, many children initially represent members of their own or some other family by separate drawings, even if they are drawn immediately after one another, but, later on, they are combined in a single drawing. Three consecutive drawings by a girl (6;8) represented a girl on her own, a boy on his own, and then a girl and boy holding hands. In the same way, houses are often suggested by drawings of people and these are often described as their house, even though they are initially drawn separately. It is only later, when they are juxtaposed on the same sheet of paper, that the child gets the idea of relating them together in the same drawing.

However, there can be no question that the major source of transformation from an original motif into a derived motif comes from those drawings which, having been drawn with the intention of representing a certain motif, are eventually given a different one. In fact, the relation thus established retrospectively between the drawing and its new interpretation is remembered by the child and provokes the intention of later drawings with the same name. The interpretation given to the drawing turns the initial drawing into a new motif derived from the originally intended motif. The child therefore believes he has already drawn this derived motif and may thus be tempted to reproduce it. This process is especially clear when children, in their attempts to produce another version of the derived drawing, are forced to recognise their lack of ability. This was the case for a young girl (4;6) who had produced a drawing she interpreted as a sheep and with which she was pleased (fig. 12). The next day she announced that she was going to draw another one, saying 'I know how to do them', but she had hardly begun before she was forced to stop and admit that she did not really know how to draw sheep.

Thus the creation of new motifs is provoked by interpretations that differ from the original intention for the drawing. Since these different interpretations are usually caused by analogies of shape arising from imperfections in the drawing, one might say that the enrichment of the child's graphic repertoire is primarily due to productive mistakes.

3
The Type

22. The 'type', by which I mean the way in which any given child represents the same object or motif over a sequence of drawings, shows a gradual development. As in all cases of development, it is the result of two factors: an element of stability ('conservation of the type'), and an element of change ('modification of the type').

Conservation of the type refers to the tendency of children to keep producing drawings of the same motif in the same way. This is a form of routine or automatism by analogy I referred to earlier in relation to motifs as graphic automatism, which can be of either an immediate (§12) or continuous kind (§13).

23. The conservation of type first appears in the form of the first drawing of a certain motif: one might call this first kind of conservation of type primary conservation. A clear example is provided by the first drawings of a man which remain cast in the same mould over a rather long period. These are distinguished by the absence of a trunk (figs 22 and 54), so that the arms, if they are shown, have to be attached either to the legs (figs 24–27) or more often to the head (figs 23, 28, 85–87, 97, 105).

Primary conservation is all the more remarkable in the case of such 'tadpole' men since the type thus conserved clearly conflicts with reality; only the effect of habit could prevent the child from noticing such striking imperfections for so long. Furthermore, the bizarre way of attaching arms to the head which this causes continues in those drawings where inclusion of the trunk no longer justifies this. The arms only gradually become correctly attached to the trunk.

But, although this is the case for man drawings where the trunk is drawn frontally, human figure drawings in profile which include the trunk generally show correct attachment of the arms from the outset. The reason for this is that human figure drawings in profile appear later, and so do not pass through the trunkless stage. Since, for these drawings, correct attachment of the arms is possible and since they, unlike human figure drawings shown entirely full face, are not constrained by an earlier type of faulty attachment, these figure drawings have the arms attached to the body from the very outset.

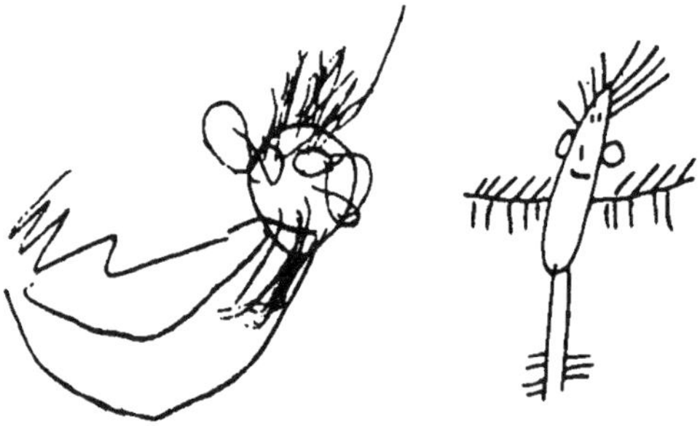

Fig. 22. Simonne Luquet, French, 3;9 (Luquet collection). A man. Human figure without trunk. The clothes were not depicted (§46) even though this characteristic of real people was indicated to her at the time (§45). Realist intention (§53–54).

Fig. 23. Bavarian girl, 7 years (after Kerschensteiner). Man without trunk and with the arms attached to the head. Multiple fingers set out all along the arms (§32). Individual hairs (§73).

24. Conservation of the type not only prevents children from noticing any improvements they could make to their drawings, but it also resists any changes suggested to them. For example, a young boy (3;10) made his first deliberate attempt to draw a man, which consisted of just a head and legs. On his sister's suggestion, he added the arms, but these were not conserved in his following drawings. Eight days later, when he boasted that he could draw as well as his sister, she objected that he did not know how to draw people with clothes on, but this suggestion had no effect on him. Various observers have reported that children continue to draw tadpole men with the arms attached to the head, even when this fault has been pointed out to them and even when they have been invited to look at themselves to see where their own arms are attached.

A young girl (5;3) asked her nurse to draw her some people, and when the nurse drew them in a way different from the girl's own type of drawings, she emphatically protested 'That is not how they are done' (meaning 'not how I do them'). After examining them

Figs 24–26. Joseph, D. French, 5 years (Luquet collection).
Men without trunks and with their arms attached to their legs (§23).
Hat in the air (§68, 73).

more closely, she seemed to accept them, but this did not prevent her from drawing her own type beside the nurse's drawings. Other cases demonstrate that for children even as old as seven-and-a-half, suggestions from other people, including those they are given at school, may sometimes have a momentary effect, yet lead to no lasting effects on their spontaneous drawings with their distinct forms.

Conservation of the type also opposes the persistence of modifications children themselves make to their types. These modifications, whether accidental or intentional, usually disappear very quickly even when they serve to bring the drawing into closer relation with the object represented, by the addition of a new detail, or by more accurate depiction of existing details or their interrelations.

Even when the innovation provides a closer relation to reality, such as the inclusion of the trunk in a man drawing, this is not maintained at first and is only definitely acquired after a rather long period of vacillation between the primitive type and the new type.

Modifications to the type can come about by accident or mere lack of skill. In such cases, there is no reason for the child to feel guilty, but even when the modifications are perfectly acceptable and their only fault is their novelty, the child feels the need to make excuses for them by coming up with some sophisticated justification, or at least points them out. Through fantasy or an error, a Californian girl (3;8) gave one of her man drawings two pairs of eyes (fig. 57), and spontaneously said: 'Two eyes at each side; that's how I do them now.' However, this anomaly did not continue in her following drawings.

Fig. 27. Michael, Belgian, 4 years (after Rouma). Man drawing without trunk and with arms inserted along the legs (§68). Fingers set out along the arms (§68).

Fig. 28. Ali, Berber, 4 years (after Probst). Man with fez. Man drawing without trunk and arms inserted in the head (§23).

This resistance to any modification of the type is most remarkable when, even though the change is an improvement, the child is only able to see it as a mistake and something to explain away. For example, a girl (3;6) drew a detail in a house which had not occurred in her previous house drawings. When asked what it was, she said that 'it's nothing at all', a stock answer (like 'it doesn't count') which for her, along with other children, amounted to an admission that she had made a mistake. However, she finally admitted that the detail was meant to be a window, but she was not happy with it because her previous ones had not included curtains. This improvement, the addition of curtains to the windows, was rejected simply because it was an innovation.

Sometimes the modification made to the type is accepted, at least for the present drawing (even if it is not conserved in the following ones) but the drawing is then completed in a way which conserves the original type. The new is given a place beside the old that it will eventually supplant. Thus a girl of six, having drawn a house with a carriage-entrance where she always drew one of the windows, moved rather than omitted this window thus disrupting the symmetry of the windows, and then explained this rearrangement by the addition of the door.

Such conservation of the old beside the new has a curious result: a single feature of an object may be drawn twice, without the child showing the least concern. For example, for many different children, when the head of their man drawing begins to be given a protuberance at one of its edges corresponding to a nose in profile, they nevertheless conserve the internal details of the full face, and include a second nose between the two eyes.

Sometimes, when the child approves of the changes, innovation triumphs over routine, but only with the help of external influences. Thus a young girl (4;8) replaced her previous drawings in which the rooms were simply juxtaposed by one where they were connected. Even though this modification in the type was an improvement in terms of the interrelation of the parts, she felt the need to justify it and, talking to herself while she was drawing, she gave the following explanation: 'This is quicker (to draw).' This explanation certainly had some truth in it, and this is probably why this change persisted in her later drawings of houses. Nevertheless, she clearly felt the need to tell herself this in order to excuse her deviation from her habitual type of house drawing.

25. The automatic nature of the conservation of type is particularly clear in those drawings where children continue to include details whose meaning they have already forgotten, so that their persistence can only be explained in terms of routine. For example, the drawings of women by one girl, since the age of three-and-a-half, had been 'crinkled', the contour of the face being drawn with curvy lines, which were meant, as she repeatedly claimed, to represent a hat. She was asked the meaning of these curvy lines about two drawings of this type which she had done at 3;7 and at 3;9. In the case of the first, she replied 'it is her hair', which was nothing more than the kind of sophisticated justification we have already noted (§3), for in earlier drawings she had included the hair. For the second drawing, she did not even bother to try to explain the 'crumpled' contour. 'It's her shape', she said. – 'But why is it like that?' – 'Because it *has* to be.' I can see no other way of putting this than 'Because that is my type [i.e., my way of doing women].'

26. As we have seen, the original type tends to remain as it had been in the initial drawing (primary conservation). This is also true of any modifications which, after some resistance from the primary type, are introduced as the result of factors to be discussed later. Other things being equal, they are conserved to the same degree.

Such secondary conservation occurs even when the modification retained is unjustified, thus clearly demonstrating its automatic nature.

For example, a girl (5;6) transferred the triangular window of her 'king's castle' first to 'rich men's houses' to symbolise their luxury (fig. 29), and then to an ordinary house where there was no longer any reason for it. This detail persisted in her subsequent drawings of houses until the final one she drew at 8;8.

Fig. 29. Simonne Luquet, French, 5;4 (Luquet collection). Wealthy house. The triangular windows come from drawings of royal castles, and the curvy edges are meant to symbolise luxury (§55 and 56).

27. Once there has been a modification of the primary type, or, in other words, the emergence of a secondary type, the latter coexists with the first and also tends to be conserved. From then on, both primary and secondary conservation compete with one another in the subsequent drawings of the same subject.

The two types can either coexist, alternating between a roughly equal number of examples, or there can be relative suppression of one of the types, so that there are just a few sporadic examples in the child's drawings of one of them and a much greater number of the other. One of the types may even completely disappear. Generally, these different outcomes of the conflict between primary and secondary conservation fluctuate over periods of variable length in drawings of the same subject. When drawing a man, one small boy (4;7) asked: 'Are the arms attached to the head or the body?', and he was told to 'Look at yourself to see how they are attached'. 'Yes', he said, 'they are on the body', and he completed his drawing by doing them this way. But, in his subsequent drawings, these two ways of attaching the arms alternated; in particular, the attachment of the arms to the head regularly appeared when the men were not drawn in isolation but as a secondary element in a more complex drawing (e.g., in a plane, or on a horse). It appears that the secondary type prevails only through an effort of attention.

28. The tendency to conserve the type is manifest not only in children's own drawings, but also in their attitude towards the drawings of others. Children insist that drawings produced at their request should always be drawn in the same way. A boy from California, in the first quarter of his fourth year, incessantly asked other people to draw horses for him, and always according to the same formula: 'a horse, a man on its back, the reins, a whip, and water for the horse to drink'. Other examples show even more clearly how children insist that anyone drawing for them should remain as faithful to their types as they are themselves. I once drew my daughter (3;6) a dog according to the type she habitually drew, and then, in order to see what she would say, I drew another one next to it and I put two eyes beside one another in the profile of the head. She protested, 'That hasn't got two eyes – That's silly! Dogs like people do have two eyes. But those you have done (until now) have only one'; and she rubbed out one of the eyes with her finger.

This rigid insistence by children is especially striking when someone else deviates from their own usual type of drawing by adopting the child's own type. For example, the same girl asked me to draw a frog, and I drew one similar to one she had done the day before. She exclaimed: 'A frog isn't like that. Well, yes, ... and no. It's not how *you* draw them.'

29. We now confront an almost incredible yet well established fact that must upset any preconceptions based on an overly simplistic conception of the minds of children. Children recognise that other people draw according to types different from their own, and, as we have seen, they insist that other people remain as faithful to their types as they do to their own. In addition, when they are drawing for someone else, they will adopt the types of that other person instead of their own. For example, a girl (8;4), having drawn a donkey as an exercise in class, made a sketch which she was evidently pleased with (fig. 30), because, after making several improvements, she then left it as it was. But when she copied it in her exercise book to show her teacher, she made various further changes such as the addition of hooves, and an essential modification involving the substitution of two nostrils for just one (fig. 31). It thus seems that she felt her teacher would prefer visual realism and wanted to give it to her, even though, when drawing for herself, she kept to intellectual realism (§77).

Figs 30 and 31. Simonne Luquet, French, 8;4 (Luquet collection). Two drawings of a donkey, first as a sketch, and then as a neat copy for her homework. Duplicity of types (§29).

The generality of this curious fact, which could be termed duplicity of types, is clearly demonstrated by all the drawings found on our walls and roads. These graffiti are produced by children of all ages, and sometimes even by adolescents and adults. Most of the children drawing these pictures have attended school, and many of the drawings have thus been drawn between classes. Yet there are a substantial number of drawings of tadpole figures (drawings of people without a trunk), which would be quite unacceptable to any teacher. One must therefore conclude that children simultaneously deploy two different types of the same motif: one is for their own personal satisfaction, and the other one is for other people.

30. If conservation of type hinders any modifications to the type, it does not completely prevent them, since all drawings of the same motif are not identical, and, furthermore, secondary conservation implies that some modifications have already occurred.

What happens is that new details are added to those that formed the earlier drawings of the same motif. This is clearly visible in the chronological succession of man drawings produced by any child.

I shall take another example of this complication of the type from the series of drawings of fronts of houses drawn by the same girl. To the original elements – door, windows, chimneys – were added in succession the name plate of the inhabitant and the bell, the step in front of the door which later became a flight of similar stairs, the lightning conductor, the balcony to which was later added a French window, the air vent and the foot-scrapers placed symmetrically on each side of the front door, its mouldings and glass fan-light, the windows ledges, the roses climbing along the walls, the tiles of the roof, the Venetian blinds with their slats, the representation of an open door and open windows, revealing a man, the hinges of the windows and of the doors. These details largely persisted in the subsequent drawings. In various examples, the house was completed with a road, which in turn came to show the same gradual addition of details: the passers-by, a man opening the door of the house with a key, the pavements, the street water supply with the lever for drawing the water, the running water, 'the spout which leads the water away into the stream' and a small girl who has come to get some water with a bucket.

31. The addition of previously absent details to the drawing of something is determined by the same factors that provoke the intention to draw an entire drawing (see §8–14). The effect of external circumstances is manifest in drawings produced on a rainy day, where the rain is shown or the people carry open umbrellas (fig. 7). In the same way, children will include a new detail if they have come across an object that happens to have it, unlike other examples they have seen before. The novelty of the feature attracts their attention. Thus in two successive drawings of houses, a girl aged a few months over four put a flag on the chimney alongside the smoke because while out for a walk she had noticed one on the chimney of a recently built house. A country girl (7;6), after a visit to Paris where she had been impressed by the tall buildings, drew a 'farm-house' with a large number of windows, and explained 'This is a house in Paris: it has a lot of windows because it has lots of storeys.' Such experiences also led her to add to her drawings of houses long flights of steps, window ledges, and roses climbing up the walls.

Modification of type can occur not only because of the novelty of actual objects, but also through drawings by other people which show the object differently from how the child would draw it. For example, a girl (6;6) and her friend were keeping themselves entertained by drawing their own portraits. The girl noticed that her friend had represented her neck, which she never included in her own drawings, and furthermore when her friend drew her fingers she had counted them and drawn five. Since the girl had, as always, only put three fingers on each hand, she swiftly added two more to each hand. After being suppressed in a series of about ten drawings of small girls produced in immediate succession, this new type then prevailed; three days later, when she was drawing alone, she drew about a dozen small girls similar to those done by her friend, and she herself attributed them to her friend and contrasted them favourably with her own earlier efforts.

As an example of a detail provoked by the association of ideas, I will refer to a drawing of a lady in the rain which suggested, by contrast, the sun shining above a horse-rider which was drawn immediately after (figs 7 and 8).

An interesting corollary of the association of ideas, either in its general form, or in the specific form of analogy of shape entails what I call transfer by analogy. When two drawings are similar or represent similar objects, the details of one may be transferred to the other. For example, the way many children attach the arms to the head in their tadpole men is carried over initially into their full-face drawings of men with a trunk. However, once they have drawn men with a trunk in profile where the arms are properly attached, this correct attachment is transferred, in turn, to full-face drawings of men with a trunk.

Sometimes such transfer by analogy gives rise not to a modification of a pre-existing type, but to the formation of a new type. This is generally the case for drawings of animals which are initially given a human appearance (figs 32 and 112); often they are really no more than man drawings, and not even always drawn horizontally. I could give limitless examples. A four-year-old Belgian boy drew two cats (fig. 33) that looked just like tadpole men endowed with gigantic tails; the one on the left seems to have two human ears plus two cat's ears which had been substituted for the first pair by tacit correction.[9] The first donkey deliberately drawn by a French girl (4;4) was an elongated human head set horizontally and put on four legs (fig. 34). This drawing failed to please her, however, because, as she stated herself, it looked too much like a man; immediately afterwards, she drew another donkey just beside the first, on which she placed a rider (fig. 35). On the other hand, a German boy of about five was pleased with how very life-like his drawing of a dog was, even though it was no more than a man drawing with two big nostrils and lines representing the fur. Children from many different countries may juxtapose a person and

9. In tacit correction, the child adds the corrections but simply treats the incorrect details as if they no longer exist and leaves them unchanged.

some animal (e.g. a dog or horse) in their drawings, but it is difficult to tell them apart, and their meaning can only be established by what the child says about them. This is especially striking in the case of six butterflies drawn in line by a French boy (6;6), where each 'butterfly' was simply a man figure endowed with a pair of circular wings with radiating lines (fig. 36).

Immediate graphic automatism gives rise to a tendency, common among children until about five, to exaggerate the number of certain

Fig. 32. Pierre R., French, 6;6 (Luquet collection). Lion. Animal derived from a man figure. Decoratively coloured (§50).

Fig. 33. Ernest, Belgian, 4 years (after Rouma). Two cats. Animal derived from a man figure.

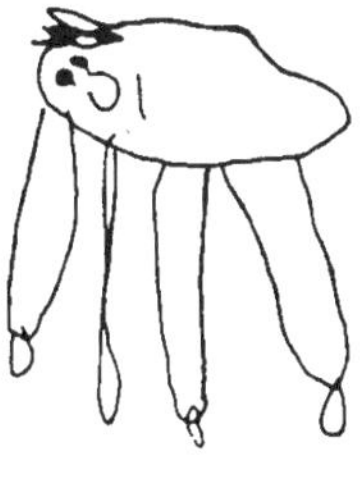

Figs 34 and 35. Jean Luquet, French, 4;6 (Luquet collection). Two consecutive drawings of a donkey, the first derived from a man figure and criticised for that reason; the second of a type really corresponding to an animal. The boy then represented himself mounted on it, in the motif of a horse and rider (§47).

Fig. 36. Jean Cr., French, 6;6 (Luquet collection). Butterfly.
Animal derived from a man figure (§31).

details of the object represented. For example, a girl (4;6) claimed to be drawing an actual church she had seen, but instead of drawing the actual number of doors in its entrance, which she had herself stated to be three, she drew half a dozen.

32. The addition of excess details as a result of the various factors already discussed, is especially striking when those details are incompatible with the overall drawing. Thus a Belgian girl (4;6), having begun to add skirts to her drawings of women, transferred them to her drawings of men, which were distinguished by still having a hat like her earlier drawings of men. In the same way, women are graced with a moustache or a pipe. One girl (as noted earlier) transferred the triangular windows of her 'royal castles', first to 'houses of rich people', where they symbolised luxury (fig. 29), then to ordinary houses where there was no reason for them. Six months later, because of their functional analogy with ordinary windows, she gave these triangular windows Venetian blinds, without her noticing that it would be impossible to close them; and nine months after that, the sky-lights in the attic were also given Venetian blinds because they had a similar shape to the triangular windows (i.e. through analogy of shape). This same girl at 7;6 put a chimney on top of a garden bower, and when this impossible feature was pointed out to her, she justified it in terms of the similarity between the bower and a house. Some buttons were added to a back

view of a cat because of the resemblance of its overall shape to that of a man. In the case of a train, the locomotive suggested a quadruped and the lantern then became its head, and was given two eyes and a mouth (fig. 14). Many children transfer the four legs of their previous animal drawings to their initial drawings of fish and birds.

In short, the multiplication of details as a consequence of graphic automatism often conflicts starkly with reality. Many children from various countries give their man drawings an impossible number of fingers (figs 18 and 23). A decisive example is that of quadrupeds (figs 89 and 112), which are often given more than four legs, and sometimes as many as 20 or more, warranting the name 'millipede' given by one five-year-old boy to one of his own drawings of this kind.

All of these examples demonstrate the labile state of mind which is so characteristic of young children (§15). When the factors which we have noted lead children to add something conflicting with the overall drawing, they do not notice its incompatibility, and more or less completely forget the initial intention of the drawing.

When these anomalies are pointed out, their attitude is the same as it is for other imperfections in their drawings (§3); in general, they resort to a rather sophisticated justification, where, without much hesitation, they calmly affirm, in one way or another, that the drawing is fine as it is. For example, an American girl (2;3) and a Belgian boy (4 years old), having drawn a mouse with too many legs, justified their drawings in the same way: 'This is to make it easier for it to save itself from the big cat.' A five-year-old Belgian boy, on being criticised for giving his chickens five, six or even seven legs, replied 'There are chickens like that; they have lots of legs.' A French girl (3;6) added two small circles which she said were wheels to the bottom of her drawing of a house, no doubt by analogy with a cart. When it was pointed out to her that houses do not have wheels, she replied 'That doesn't matter.'

33. In the different examples we have considered so far, the elaboration of the type is the result of a synthetic process rather like sedimentation. The details introduced into a drawing of a motif are gathered from elsewhere, coming either from new examples of the actual object, or from drawings of that same object by other people, or from other objects, even if these details are at times incompatible with what is being drawn. However, another way the type becomes elaborated comes from within the drawing itself, through a process of analysis analogous to the differentiation of a developing

Figs 37–44. Simonne Luquet, French, 7 years (Luquet collection).
Seven consecutive drawings of Gayant and Madame Gayant.
Faithful to the memory which provoked the intention (§8).
There is a 'growth' in the type across the series of drawings (§33).

organism. For this reason, I refer to it as the 'growth' of the type. It is as though the overall representation of the object 'blossoms' through the successive development of details which it can no longer control.

I will take as an example a series of houses with their rooms in plan view drawn by the same girl and inspired by the same actual object, her own house. The entire house, first pictured in elevation, and then in plan view, gave birth successively, through a kind of budding, to the toilet, the kitchen, the bedroom, the laundry, the dining room, the study, and the bathroom. Then each of these rooms was in turn elaborated by new details. Thus, in the dining room, the table, which was at first the only object shown, was joined by the sideboard, and then the chairs. In the kitchen, the stove and sideboard were joined by the utensil rack, the table with the maid's plate, and the chair. Then, in turn, details were added to the furniture: for example, in the kitchen, the stove acquired the tap of the boiler, legs and ovens, and, on the table, a bottle and glass appeared beside the plate. To the house itself was added a courtyard,

Fig. 45. Gayant and Madame Gayant (after a photograph): the subject of the drawings in figures 37–44.

which later divided into a court and a garden, with each acquiring several details: walls, flowerbeds, trees, and flowers.

The same process of differentiation in the growth of the type is very clear in the development of two analogous details: the pipe or cigarette in man drawings and the chimneys of houses. At first, the cigarette and its smoke are first shown by a single form, represented by a curvy line, but these later become separated, and the cigarette is then shown by a straight line and the smoke by a winding line extending from its end. Then the differentiation goes even further: the wavy line representing the smoke is added afterwards, by a separate stroke of the pen, to the straight line depicting the cigarette. In addition, the line representing the cigarette is itself distinct and added to a separate line for the mouth, whereas formerly the same line had represented both the mouth and the cigarette. It is the same for the chimneys of houses. First, both the chimney and its smoke are shown by a single zigzag trace, depicting the chimney and smoke as an undifferentiated whole, which is later substituted by a straight line for the chimney, extended by a kind of ball representing the smoke. Then the straight line representing the chimney is replaced by a rectangular shape.

An especially clear example of this process of differentiation is provided by the series of drawings by a seven-year-old girl representing Gayant, the legendary giant from the town of Douai (figs 37–45). The first two drawings show the body and the cloak, the head with no details and the two sides of the helmet, the crest with its feathers; the third also includes the features of the face; the fourth and fifth, the decorated round shield with a gothic 'd' which serves as the arms of the town of Douai; the sixth the lance and the hand which is holding it; the seventh, the coat of mail and the armour for the thighs.

The reason I have drawn upon this rather special example is that such drawings, produced immediately after one another and drawn from the memory of a single visual experience, allow us to see the growth of the type in its clearest form: the child when drawing the first example already knows about those details which nevertheless only appear in the later ones. It is just the same in the much more general case of man drawings, where the type gradually acquires, for all children, a growing number of details. The trunk, the arms, the clothes, the hair, and the neck, each appear in a relatively constant sequence. Then each of these elements in turn develops on its own account. The legs, for example, become differentiated into legs and feet and then each of these is no longer shown as a simple line, but as a contour; and the eyes are given pupils and eyebrows. Clearly, although their earliest man drawings are formed solely by a circle for the head and two roughly parallel lines (and sometimes just one) for the legs, it is by no means the case that children are unaware of the other features of the body, at least the more noticeable ones, even when they do not include them in the drawings.

4
The Internal Model

34. So far I have been considering how the type (i.e. the distinctive way a child draws a particular subject) comes to be both conserved and modified. The type is not an artificial abstraction, a mere label we apply to a set of similar drawings of the same motif by the same child. It corresponds to something psychologically real within the mind of the child: the *internal model*. It is this that evokes in children's minds the representation of the object and the intention to draw it, and even when these are suggested by the sight of an object or a model, the resulting drawing is not, as one might assume, a mere copy. The object being drawn, before it can be translated onto the paper, necessarily takes the form of a visual image. However, this image is by no means the slavish reproduction of any of the perceptions afforded the artist by a view of the object or by a corresponding drawing. It is a refraction of the object to be drawn through the mind of the child, a creative, though spontaneous, reconstruction arising from an extremely complex process of elaboration. The term 'internal model' is meant to distinguish the object or model in the strict sense from this mental representation which is expressed in the drawing.

35. When a drawing is produced from memory, or as they say in the studios, *de chic* ('without a model'), then it is necessarily based upon the internal model. But it is also the internal model that children copy even when they explicitly declare that they are reproducing something in front of them, that is, drawing from nature or copying from other drawings. In both these cases, the external object merely serves as a suggestion but what is really being drawn is the internal model. The proof of this is that drawings from nature and also copies of other drawings have the same characteristics as drawings from memory, the most fundamental feature being that they conform not to visual realism but to intellectual realism (§71).

For example, in some drawings from actual objects, a bell (fig. 46) is shown with its clapper even though in reality it was invisible since the bell was standing on the table, and a bobbin (fig. 47) is shown from three different viewpoints: in profile for the central cylinder, and 'face on' for each of the two round, pierced ends. The view of a penknife on the table on which a girl (3;6) was drawing provoked her intention to draw it, but, instead of the actual penknife in front of her, her drawing reproduced the 'intelligible' penknife, in the Platonic sense. The penknife had two blades, and both were closed and hence were not visible. But her drawing depicted an open penknife with a single blade. The drawing of a vase of flowers from nature (figs 81–83) is particularly revealing, since the child had constantly looked at the object (fig. 84) 'in order to create a resemblance'. This did not prevent the rings at the side of the vase from being drawn according to intellectual realism. The generality of the fact that, when drawing from nature, children do not copy the actual object but their internal model is confirmed by experiments conducted on school children, notably in America and Bavaria. For example, when school children were asked to draw the teacher's desk, nearly all of them included the drawers with their handles, even though these were on the side of the desk they could not see.

Figs 46 and 47. Simonne Luquet, French, 7;6 (Luquet collection). Bell and bobbin. The intervention of the internal model in drawings from nature (§35).

36. Copies of drawings also show the effect of the internal model. In such drawings, two cases need to be distinguished: when the copy is faithful, and when it is not. Now it can be faithful either when the model copied by children is like one they would have themselves have drawn based on their own internal models of the depicted object, or else when the model they are copying is unfamiliar to them because of its overall shape or some of its details. In the latter case, they do not transform it because they do not understand it. For example, when I expressed my regret to a young boy (4;4) that he had rubbed out a drawing on the wall by his sister before I could copy it, he told me he would do it again for me. His reproduction

from memory (fig. 49) was extremely accurate: it included the carriage with its two wheels, the horse, the driver and the reins; and yet when I asked him what this drawing represented, he said he had no idea.

Fig. 48. Seven-year-old German girl (after Levinstein). Man drawing with arms inserted into the head, even though it has a trunk (§23).

Fig. 49. Jean L., French, 4;6 (Luquet collection). Horse and carriage. Faithful copy of a drawing which made no sense to the child (§36).

In contrast, when children understand the model upon which they are basing their own drawing, and this differs from their own internal model of the depicted object, it is not the model as such that is drawn but their internal model. The earliest man drawings produced by many children are inspired by examples drawn by their parents or their older brothers and sisters, yet they bear no resemblance to those drawings and are nearly always drawn without a trunk. In two drawings copied from the same picture of a house drawn by girl a year apart, the vertical chimney was replaced by one perpendicular to the slope of the roof, as a result of the confusion of vertical and perpendicular that occurs among many different children in their drawings without a model, such as the chimneys of houses (fig. 94), or people or trees shown on the side of a mountain. The drawing in figure 50 is especially instructive because of its close relation to its model, taken from a magazine. Its subject, as understood by the child, was as follows: two dirigible balloons were passing in the sky and a gentleman, perched on a roof among the chimneys, was waiting for them with his cane and his suitcase. The logical elements of this picture are: two dirigible balloons, the clouds, the chimneys, a kind of platform supporting a man who was holding a cane and a suitcase. The modifications introduced by the child in her copy all serve to make these logical elements more evident than they were in the original model. The smaller dirigible, partly obscured by a cloud in the original, is entirely separated from it in the copy; it is sufficient to show the clouds underneath. The chimneys are incidental, and are reproduced accordingly by simple marks, so that one knows they are there. What is more revealing, however, is the way the representation of the gentleman has been modified. In the original model, he was facing the dirigibles and hence, in accord with the visual realism that guides the drawings of the adult, he is necessarily shown in profile. But this disturbs the child, since in a representation in profile the different elements – the body, the arms, the cane and the case – more or less occlude one another. Instead, she replaced this representation in profile by a frontal representation, both sides being changed so that the arms held out the items they are carrying to make them more clearly visible.

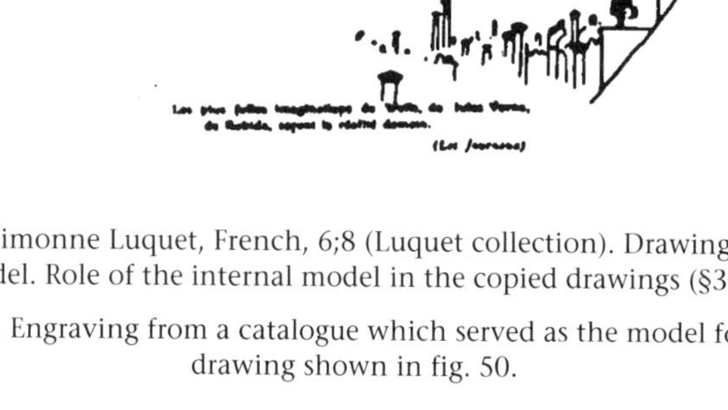

Fig. 50. Simonne Luquet, French, 6;8 (Luquet collection). Drawing from a model. Role of the internal model in the copied drawings (§36).

Fig. 51. Engraving from a catalogue which served as the model for the drawing shown in fig. 50.

37. If proof is still needed for the existence of the internal model in the minds of children and its role in their drawing, this can be found in the fact that graphic ambiguity is a factor not only in the interpretation of a drawing but also its initial intention. Now, when graphic ambiguity determines the execution of a drawing, it necessarily precedes the act of drawing. Hence graphic ambiguity must relate not to the drawing itself (which is yet to be produced) but to the internal model. When children are asked to draw something, this leads them to think of the corresponding object, and this idea then serves as the intention to reproduce this same subject. The intention and the internal model of the motif normally coincide. However, it can happen that through analogy of shape between the internal model of the intended object and that of another object, the child's mind shifts from the first to the second object with the result that the latter is then drawn.

38. Since what is drawn on the paper is the reproduction, not of the sensation or visual image of the object being drawn, but of the corresponding internal model, when children draw an object for the first time, they must first create its internal model in their minds. However, when the intention of this drawing is weak, which can happen if it is not spontaneous but provoked by an instruction, the child usually prefers to avoid the effort of generating an internal model. This explains why, when children are asked to draw something they have never drawn before, they will often try to avoid the task, and offer instead to do something they themselves know how to draw. One has really to persist in order to obtain the drawing, and then not always with success. And yet should the child produce the drawing the result is not noticeably inferior to their other drawings.

This observation relates to the view that children, in their unconscious choice of what motifs to draw, are guided by how difficult it is to produce (§9). Usually this difficulty is assumed to be graphic in nature, namely, the difficulty of drawing the corresponding lines. But one cannot assume, simply on the basis of the lines themselves, that one drawing is more difficult to produce than another, and even if this difficulty could be determined for adults, it hardly follows that it would be the same for the child. Furthermore, children can only discover this difficulty after the event, in the light of their success or failure. Many examples demonstrate that, when the child has the intention of drawing any object, this intention is realised in the corresponding drawing, no matter how imperfect its execution. The difficulty that stands in the way of the execution of an initial drawing is not graphic in nature, but mental: it is nothing other than mental laziness that causes children to avoid the effort of creating the corresponding internal model.

39. Once the initial drawing has obliged the child to create the internal model, the child keeps this in mind in so far as he continues to draw the same subject. Thus, if the child has not drawn for a rather long time, he may forget the internal model. He then finds himself in the same position he was in with the initial drawing and no longer knows how to draw the object. Some trial and error is then needed either to revive the former internal model or to create a new one, if his conception of the object has since changed.

40. The internal model intervenes not only in the production of the drawing, but also in the meaning the child gives to it. It is through their analogy with his internal models that the child interprets other people's drawings, and also his own drawings either in the course of production or after they have been completed. Children apply an interpretation that differs from their initially declared intention for two reasons. Firstly, when the resulting drawing seems to conform better to another internal model. Secondly, when their internal model of a certain subject has changed (or, in other words, there has been a modification in the type), so that they are no longer able to recognise their earlier drawings of a more primitive type.

41. How then does the internal model, which is reproduced in drawings of a particular subject, arise in the mind of the child? In order to answer this question, it will help to distinguish different kinds of motif according to their level of generality. First of all, there are 'historically situated representations'[10] which depict a definite object, seen at a certain time, in specific and sometimes unique circumstances: this could be an individual in a special setting, doing something, clothed in specific garments, in a certain place at a certain time, and where this event happens just the once. At a higher degree of generality or abstraction, the image no longer corresponds to a particular time and place, but to a certain object at any time: this would still be said to be a portrait but not an instantaneous one. Then, at an even higher degree of abstraction, individual differences would also be left out. Instead of a drawing representing a particular

10. *'représentations historiques'*

girl, for example, it would be of any girl, or even a person whose sex and age were unspecified; or instead of a marguerite or a rose, it would represent a flower, etc.

Needless to say such neat distinctions are never so clear in practice. An instantaneous photograph that captures a person at a precise moment nevertheless usually serves a more general role in representing that person as opposed to someone else. Similarly, a drawing of a particular entity could be an individual image turned to more general use, for example, when a portrait of a person comes to represent human beings in general. These different categories of motifs should be regarded, therefore, as no more than stages along a continuum from the individual to the more general. Furthermore, they intermingle, so that the same drawing might be much more specific than another in some respects and very general in others. Take, for example, two drawings by the same child: one representing his own portrait, and the second an anonymous man. The first would be more specific in relation to humanity, but it could be more general in relation to action, if the child merely gives it a neutral posture, whereas that given to the man might be a specific movement or represent a definite occupation, such as fishing with a rod. We will restrict ourselves, therefore, to making a broad distinction among drawings at two ends of a continuum: individual subjects or motifs, on the one hand, and generic motifs, on the other.

42. Especially at the outset, children's drawings usually depict generic rather than individual images. As a general rule, a generic drawing does not depend on an internal model of its own. There is nothing about its traces to distinguish it from an individual drawing, but, instead, its generality lies solely in the fact that either before or after drawing it the child does not call it daddy, for example, but a man. In other words, the child selects just one out of all the individual images of objects of a certain kind, and naturally that of which he has had the most recent experience as representative of that class. We shall give the term 'exemplarity' to this attribution of a general significance to the internal model of an individual object. For example, although the drawings of houses drawn by the same child are almost always called 'a house' (of no particular kind), the details shown, and sometimes even her comments, prove that it is inspired by her own house; thus, when drawing some of the details, she says 'like our home'. A highly typical example comes from a nine-year-old German girl. She had drawn a picture that took the form of a quadruped in profile blessed with the full-face head of a

human (like the one in fig. 34). When asked what animal it was, the question took her by surprise and she replied completely nonplussed: 'Well, an animal!' Thus her drawing claimed to depict the general idea of animal, or at least that of a quadruped.

43. Alongside exemplarity, another process intervenes in the generation of the internal model of generic motifs, and we shall call it synthesis. Putting aside the combination of already existing generic internal models (§21), this involves the combination within a single image of either the whole or the parts of various individual images which themselves derive either from a real object or from a drawing produced earlier by the child or by someone else. For example, until about the age of three-and-a-half, one girl's internal model of a house was comprised solely of details of drawings of houses drawn for her at her request, namely the facade, the roof and the windows. To them she added new elements, curtains in the windows, which she borrowed neither from other drawings nor from a real house, but from another real object, a construction kit in which the windows consisted of a frame of wood containing a pane of glass on which were painted red curtains drawn open by loops. At 5;3, in several drawings of a bedroom shown either on its own or as part of an entire house, she reproduced through exemplarity details of her parents' bedroom. However, at the same time, she also introduced into the fireplace, through synthesis, two andirons 'with the heads of babies' which had caught her attention in the house of a friend (fig. 52). A little later, when drawing a church from the town where she lived, she very carefully reproduced its external details, and especially 'the windows with the men in colour' (i.e. the stained-glass windows), and also the rope of the bell and the bell ringer who was pulling it. Nevertheless she also added a flag which had never belonged to this church but must have been borrowed from some other building, perhaps even another church (fig. 75). At five-and-a-half, this same girl added a new element to the usual details of her houses, a gable roof with a chimney at the side, which she borrowed from an illustration of a house that she had seen in a book and copied. When she was almost six, two of her drawings of houses, inspired by the seaside villa in which she was then staying, attached a garden whose details were those of her grandmother's situated far away, and which, furthermore, was not attached to her grandmother's house.

As one can see from these different examples, the type comes to be elaborated through the influence of external circumstances and

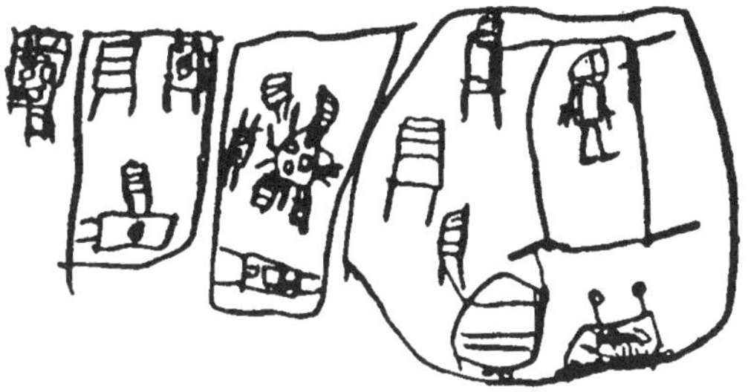

Fig. 52. Simonne Luquet, French, 5;4 (Luquet collection). House. Synthesis of the details of the bedroom (§43). Discontinuity between contiguous rooms (§68). Rabattement (§75).

analogical transfer (§31–32), and this elaboration is nothing other than the translation onto paper of the enrichment of the internal model through synthesis.

44. We now turn to the internal model of an individual as opposed to generic model. The construction of the internal model involves a creative mental act, an unconscious elaboration of material yielded by experience, namely, visual impressions of the actual object or a picture of it, which are retained in memory. This elaboration occurs in the form of a selection, a choice between the different components of the object represented. Each of these elements is just as real as the rest, and they are all equally visible. However, unlike a camera registering everything in front of its lens, the minds of children distinguish between essential and incidental details, or, to be more precise, they impose a veritable hierarchy upon them. When perceiving and remembering, the mind is not just an inert recipient that relays and conserves experiences, 'the data', just as they are. Every individual mind, and not just special kinds of mentality, can be compared to a resonator or filter that responds only to certain wavelengths. As Spinoza once said, if a peasant, a painter, and a general were to look at the same scene, they would not receive the same impressions. Similarly, a child in front of an object or drawing does not see the same details as an adult, or, more precisely, although his eyes see them, the mind perceives them only to the extent that they are of interest or given some significance by the child.

The relative importance children give to the different elements of an object is reflected by the place they are given in their drawings.

A first way of determining the hierarchy of values associated with the different details of an object is to observe which ones are included in the initial drawing of a motif. On the basis of the criticisms children make of their own drawings (§3), it is immediately possible to tell once they have stopped drawing whether they are satisfied with the drawing and regard it as a success. If this is the case, then one can infer that those details that have not been represented are regarded as unnecessary and hence secondary.

Another indication of the relative importance of the different elements of an object for the child is the emphasis they are given across a series of drawings of the same subject. As we have already seen (§33), the most important factor in the modification of the type and hence of the internal model is the progressive addition of ever more details. The chronological order in which these details appear indicates their relative importance. The more important ones appear first, and the less important ones only appear in the later drawings.

However, once a detail has appeared, either in the initial or later drawings of a certain subject, it is not the case that it is invariably conserved in all the subsequent ones. We have already seen this in relation to the conflict between primary and secondary conservation (§27). However, automatism is not the sole reason for this, or rather its role is limited to revealing and determining the characteristic we are now considering. The details included in each of the drawings are those that stand out most clearly in the internal model expressed in the drawing. The various internal models can be compared to photographic images in which only certain details, and not always the same ones, are in focus. Thus, the relation between a sequence of drawings of the same subject allows us, as in Galton's analogous method of composite images,[11] to identify those elements which the child considers to be essential, by showing which details can be left out without affecting the child's satisfaction with the drawing.

These different sources of evidence yield complementary and consistent results. I have already mentioned (§33) the definite order

11. The method of composite portraits, devised by Francis Galton (1822–1911), involved superimposing the portraits of different people photographically to eliminate their individual peculiarities and bring out, as he put it, 'their common humanity'. The technique was used by Galton to try to capture the facial appearances of different criminal and racial 'types'. [Francis Galton (1878). Composite portraits made by combining those of many different persons into a single figure, *Journal of the Anthropological Institute, 8,* 132–48.]

in which most children's drawings of men are elaborated and completed by the addition of new details. Similarly, most drawings of a front view of a house remain for some time without a roof. Occasionally, in drawings of various children, the contour of the face is either limited to its upper half, which might represent the forehead, or else it is totally absent. One girl, in her plan drawings of houses, often left out the outline either of the whole house or the rooms, and only represented their furniture. Sometimes she used the same outline to represent both a room and one of its pieces of furniture. For example, in two of her drawings drawn at 4;4, the study was depicted by an outline shape which represented both the walls, since it contained a door and windows, but, at the same time, it also represented the table, since it was given legs.

45. Within the hierarchy in which children place the elements of any drawn object, they seem to make a fundamental distinction between merely secondary and incidental details (even if some are more important than others) and the essential element which constitutes, to use the appropriate metaphysical term, its substance. The proof lies in the fact that when children announce the details of a drawing they often do not mention this substantial element, as though it were not a detail like the others, but the support for them. For example, when listing the elements of their houses, children mention the door, the windows, the chimney, but not the outline of the facade (§24). At other times, this essential detail is given the name of the object itself. For example when drawing a rabbit, they refer to its different parts in the following way: the rabbit (its body), the head, the feet and the tail. Similarly, a four-year-old Californian girl was listing the elements of a watch as she was drawing them: 'This is the watch, this is the hand, and this is the thing on the side [the ring for attaching the watch chain]' (fig. 53).

Although it would clearly be an exaggeration to claim that children deliberately leave out some of the details of the real object they are drawing, it has to be said that they are conscious to some extent of the existence of those elements even when they are neglecting them. A clear example comes from a man drawn by a girl (3;9) (fig. 22). Even though he was given no arms, trunk, or clothes, she regarded it with evident satisfaction, which she expressed as follows: 'That's good; he's such a smartly dressed man.' Even though she was leaving out the clothes in her drawings she nevertheless invoked these to characterise a real man.

Fig. 53. Ruth W., Californian, 4 years (after Brown).
Watch (a. watch; b, hand; c, movement of the hand on the dial; d, winder, e, chain). Example of the substance, and of graphic narrative (§83).

Fig. 54. Caroll, Californian boy (3;6) (after Brown).
Man without trunk (§23). One arm detached from body (§68).

46. As we shall see (§71), children not only insist upon including all those elements they regard as essential in their drawing of any object, even when they are not visible, but, conversely, they also leave out those they consider to be secondary, even when they are visible. It is perhaps possible to go even further and try to get some better understanding of why children attribute different levels of importance to the different elements of an object. The child is essentially a 'teleologist', in the Socratic sense. The child's representation of things is, to use Renan's term, 'anthropocentric'. A young girl used to refer to things exclusively according to their role, not their name. A chair was 'a to-sit-on', a plate, 'a to-eat-from'. Once, in an attempt to catch her out, I pointed to a slug and asked her: 'What's that then?' I felt rather sheepish when she replied: 'That's a to-stamp-on.' Without wishing to suggest that all children take their teleological outlook this far, I do believe that they are powerfully inspired by it, and that the relative importance they attach to the different details of an object depends in large part on the role or function they attribute to them.

For example, it is well known that at first all children draw their men with no clothes on (figs 22, 109, 142), even when they represent grown-ups, whom the children have never ever seen naked. If it is the case that their knowledge of nudity comes from having seen themselves with no clothes on, why should this have more influence upon them than that of their clothed body which, after all, is certainly a more frequent experience? Certainly, the clothes are not indispensable to the nature of a human being and they may even detract from its representation since they conceal and in a sense suppress the otherwise essential elements. The clothes are not even necessary for characterising the gender of the person, since it is enough to add a pipe for the men, a bun of hair for the women, and a pigtail for little girls. For some children, and for some period, women are characterised, not by a skirt, but by hat feathers. One five-year-old boy, having drawn a person, was asked if it was a man or a woman. Without even looking back at the drawing, he asked 'Has it got feathers?'

I will now turn to the intrinsic parts of the body. When the ears make their first appearance, it is usually only in the drawings of women. Men can do without them because they do not wear earrings. Similarly, man drawings lack arms for a very long time (figs 130 and 133), and when they do appear it is usually because the people need them because they are holding something. Furthermore, if just one arm is necessary, the other, unused one is left out, as in a drawing by a girl of five of someone opening the door of his house with a key, and a range of drawings by Munich school children representing a snowball fight (fig. 55). Sometimes, the utility of the arms in a particular drawing is not sufficient to counteract their habitual neglect, as in the drawing of a wedding (fig. 56) where most of the people arranged as couples are deprived of arms even though they need them to hold one another's hands, or a drawing of a man picking cherries by a boy (4;4) which showed a man without arms beside the cherry tree (fig. 58). The same absence of arms occurs in drawings of people playing a trumpet or carrying an open umbrella; the trumpet is held in the mouth, and the umbrella is planted on top of the head. The effect of habit is so strong that even when such drawings include people with and without arms, even those given arms still do not take hold of the objects (figs 60 and 61). One drawing by a Belgian boy (4;6) combines all the possible cases (fig. 62): it shows three couples each sheltering under their shared umbrellas. The couple on the left do not have arms and the umbrella is holding itself up. In the two other couples, one arm of each person holds the umbrella, but the non-functional arm is left out except for the person at the very right. Even when the child has come consistently to include the arms, the way they are represented is very sketchy and careless for quite a long period: each arm is represented by just a single stroke, even though the legs are by then depicted by a closed contour (figs 109 and 132).

Fig. 55. Bavarian girl, 6 years (after Kerschensteiner). People throwing snowballs. Representation of a single arm (§46) and exaggeration of its length (§67).

Fig. 56. Simonne Luquet, French, 6 years (Luquet collection). Wedding. Absence of functional arms (§46). Attempt at realistic colouring (§50). Intellectual realism (§73).

Fig. 57. Ruth W., Californian, 3;9 (after Brown). Portrait of her father, drawn by request: a bit of the arms, lungs, stomach, its 'mechanism', the other part of the stomach, its 'mechanism', eyes, nose, mouth, chin, neck. Justification of an unusual detail (§24). Depiction by transparency of the viscera (§74), which probably gave rise to the representation of the trunk (§46).

In the drawing mentioned earlier of a walk in the snow (fig. 62), the snow is shown only above the walkers since it would have no function anywhere else.

The role of finality in the choice of details is manifest throughout children's drawings of men without trunks (§23), which are the most consistent and curious of their productions. If they continue to omit the trunk for such a long time, it cannot be that they have failed to notice something so large, or have never been encouraged by others to add it. They simply do not see its point. Of course, the trunk does serve to contain the vital internal organs, but since children are usually ignorant about anatomy, they know nothing about this. This conclusion is supported by an exception to the rule, the sole example I have encountered during all my systematic studies of children's first attempts at drawing. A young Californian girl (3;4) gave her man drawings a trunk from the very outset. Inside the trunk, she drew a scribble for the 'tummy', which she named as she was drawing it. Three months later, in a portrait of her father, she drew and named the lungs, the stomach, and 'the machine that makes our stomach go: pump, pump, and the other bit of the stomach with its machine' (fig. 57). Clearly her knowledge of anatomy and physiology was somewhat far-fetched, but nevertheless the fact that the trunk was the container for 'machines', however odd, made it well worth representing for her.

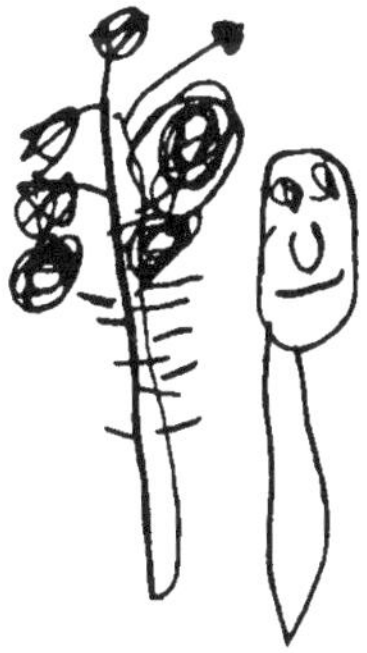

Fig. 58. Jean Luquet, French, 4;4 (Luquet collection). Man gathering cherries. Absence of even functional arms (§46).

Fig. 59. Simonne Luquet, French, 7;3 (Luquet collection). Yellow marguerite. Realistic colouring of plants (§50).

Their finalistic outlook not only explains the initial absence of the trunk in children's drawings of people, but also its eventual appearance. If they continue to remain unaware of the function of the trunk for real flesh-and-blood, nevertheless they do come to see that drawn men need them in order to connect with the arms. When the arms first make their appearance, having been initially ignored, the absence of the trunk is still maintained for a while through conservation of the type, and the child copes by attaching them either to the legs or to the head (§23). For children from many different countries, one finds in the series of their drawings of tadpole men that sometimes arms are inserted into the head and at other times into the legs. In drawings in which there are two people, both kinds of insertion can sometimes occur. Examples even exist, such as a man drawn by a Californian girl (3;6) where one of the arms is attached to the head, and the other to the legs. The vacillation in the same child between these different ways of attaching the arms proves that they are already to some extent aware of its limitations, and it is this which leads them to draw the trunk, since it is essential for the correct way of attaching the arms.

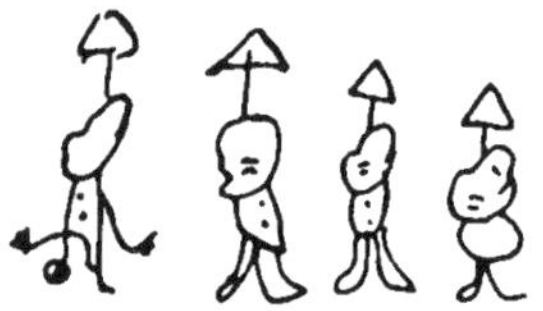

Fig. 60. Emile, Belgian, 3;6 (after Rouma). Men carrying umbrellas. Disregard for the arms (§46).

Fig. 61. Marie, Belgian, 5;6 (after Rouma). Army conscripts playing the trumpet. Disregard for the arms (§46).

47. Exemplarity, whose role we have considered in relation to the internal model of generic drawings, is also involved in individual

drawings or portraits.[12] This should not be surprising since, after all, an individual object or creature is already general in a sense. It is the sum of the different moments of its existence, and, more specifically, the diversity of its visual appearances, resulting either from any changes it has undergone or from changes in the position from which it is viewed. Among all these equally valid aspects, children spontaneously choose with impressive regularity that which best distinguishes the object in question from any others, either by its overall shape, or by its visible details. Thus the drawings of animals are consistently in profile. In contrast, people are shown exclusively from the front for a long time. This consistent choice of different points of view for representing people and animals is very clear indeed in drawings of people on horses, where the horse is in profile and the rider full-face (figs 35, 89, 100). Even later, when children are able to draw people in profile and hence are not discouraged because they are difficult to draw, profiles remain exceptional even as parts of pictures that require this point of view, such as drawings of a woman pushing a child in a pram, where the woman ought to be in profile along with the pram, or drawings of horse-riders, where the rider ought to be in profile just like the horse.

Exemplarity also plays a role in the graphic representation of unfolding scenes, or stories. Among the successive moments or episodes of the action, the child selects one or several in preference to all the others. For example, in the story of John Nose-in-the-Air, John being approached by the dog is shown more often than John tripping over the dog, and John going by the river is shown more often than John falling into the water. Those authors who have commented on this fact have concluded that the catastrophe is less often depicted than its antecedents, and have offered various explanations, notably, that the catastrophe only refers to itself, whereas what leads up to it not only represents itself but also suggests the idea of the imminent catastrophe, and is thus 'richer'. While this explanation may have some value in relation to highly experienced artists, it seems too subtle to be applied to children. In

12. Luquet uses the single term 'exemplarity' to refer both to the use of a specific image of an object to represent its general class, and also to the use of a particular view of an individual object or one of its parts as most characteristic or distinctive. I have translated this latter sense as 'exemplarity of form'. This concept is similar to what other writers on children's drawings and pictorial representation call 'canonical form'.

Fig. 62. Pierre B., Belgian, 4;6 (after Rouma). Walk in the snow. Intention provoked by external circumstances (§7). Representation of arms (§46). Role of finality (§46).

the absence of verbal confirmation from the child, there is nothing to prove that what the adult eye takes to be solely a representation of the preparation phase, is not intended by the child to depict the antecedents and the catastrophe together. But even if we can assume that the child makes a clear distinction between these two successive phases of the event, and represents the first rather than the second, the reason, in my view, is that in the latter the different logical elements of the activity are visually confused and incomplete. For example, in the representation of John tripping over the dog, the two characters are less distinct than when John is approaching it; and in the representation of John falling into the water, the part of his body immersed in the water is no longer visible, whereas if he is represented when he is still on the bank of the river just before he falls, he can be shown completely. In representations of changing scenes as in representations of static objects, the principle of exemplarity favours those drawings where visual realism and intellectual realism are in harmony.

5
Use of Colour

48. There are diverse opinions and little precise information about the attention children pay to colour in their drawings. Extensive observations of various children have yielded discrepant data, and the single overall finding is that there are large individual differences among children in their use of colour. Consequently, the conclusions presented in this chapter should be regarded as tentative.

49. Children's interest in colour in itself is related to the fact that, in a good number of their drawings, colour serves a purely decorative or ornamental role, independent of the object depicted. Colour is (to use a child's expression) 'for making things pretty'. The fronts of houses and the clothes of people provide many such examples. Thus in a self-portrait by a girl just a little over eight (fig. 63), the evident care for realism shown in the lines contrasts strikingly with the purely decorative use of colour (the hat is brimstone yellow even though it was not a straw hat, the bodice is green and the skirt is purple). In a man drawing by a boy (4;3), the contour of the head is in black, the nose and arms are red, and one eye is violet and the other green. In another drawing, a month later, the contour of the head, and the legs and one arm are red, but the other arm is blue, the details of the face are brown, and the fingers are red, blue and brown. In coloured drawings of railway trains, the locomotive is usually covered in a host of unlikely colours, such as a green body, an orange chimney and smoke, a violet driver's cabin, and a blue tender. One can observe this tendency to use colour decoratively in relation to those colouring books where an already coloured example is presented on the page facing an outline copy for the child to fill in with colours. For example, a boy (6;3) colouring a bicycle according to a model with light grey tyres, coloured one of them maroon and the other green. In drawings without a model by the same child, decorative colouring was applied not only to houses as well as to fishing and pleasure boats, where such decoration might be regarded

as having some basis in reality, but also to the walls of barracks and forts and to the hulls of warships.

Fig. 63. Simonne Luquet, French, 8;2 (Luquet collection). Self-portrait. Coloured caption (§84). Decorative colouring of clothing (§49) and realistic colouring of the cheeks (§50).

Fig. 64. Simonne Luquet, French, 5;6 (Luquet collection). Doll. Intellectual realism (§73).

50. Given the dominant role of realism in children's drawings in the rendition of shape (chapter 6), we should not be surprised to find that colour, besides its decorative function, also has a realist role.

There is some logic to how these two different roles are deployed. Colour is used decoratively when it is just an accidental feature of the represented object, that is, when that object could have a different colour, as in the case of clothes. In contrast, it is realistic when the colour is essential to the object. This occurs for representations of certain objects that have always had that colour, or had it at the time it was drawn. For example, the drawing of a 'pop-gun' faithfully reproduced the coloured red and green bands (fig. 66), and a girl, in a portrait of her mother from life, was just as precise in rendering the red colour of her dressing gown (red) as its style (fig. 67). In the drawing of a concert (fig. 68), mainly in black ink, the scene with the performer of the monologue was drawn in red ink 'because the curtains are red' (i.e. they were red in the original scene). When drawing a wedding (fig. 56), a six-year-old girl only had a red and blue pencil, but she wanted to depict the white dress of the

Fig. 65. Simonne Luquet, French, 7;3 (Luquet collection). Piano. Multi-coloured signature (§48). Mixture of realistic and decorative colouring (§50).

bride. With this intention in mind, she drew all the other characters in red, but the bride with her veil with a blue pencil.

Fig. 66. Simonne Luquet, French, 7;2 (Luquet collection). Pistol. Realistic colouring (§50).

Turning from drawings of individual objects and portraits, to generic images, colour is as essential as shape when all of the objects of that kind regularly have the same colouring. In such cases, the

Fig. 67. Simonne Luquet, French, 7;1 (Luquet collection). Portrait of her mother in a garland of roses. Realistic representation of her clothing and its colour (§50).

colouring of the drawing is generally realistic, but with one important exception. In the case of animals there is a definite predilection for decorative colouring. For example, in some drawings by the same girl, a meadow attached to a house included, at 7;6, a blue sheep, a violet dog, and a greenish-yellow hen; at 8;2, a bird with a green head, a red body, and blue wings and tail, and yellow beak and legs (fig. 69); and, most strikingly, at 8;6, a swan with a deep green body, bright yellow wings and a brown tail (fig. 71). In drawings by a boy from the age of six until he was six-and-a-half, I came across a yellow dog, and another one with a brown body, red ears, a green eye, violet tail; an elephant seen foreshortened from behind, with a yellow-brown trunk, red head and ears, and a blue bottom; an amazing lion (fig. 32) with a red body, yellow-brown tail and green mane. I can find no very satisfying explanation why animals are given this decorative colouring; perhaps children think of fur and feathers as kinds of animal clothing and then transfer the decorative colouring they give to human clothes to them.

In contrast to animals, the examples I have seen of plants are regularly painted in realistic colours, such as a water-reed (fig. 72) and two marguerites (figs 59 and 107). The sky and streams of water are consistently blue (fig. 74); flags, by French children, are always in tricolour. In a drawing of a church, the flag was the only detail

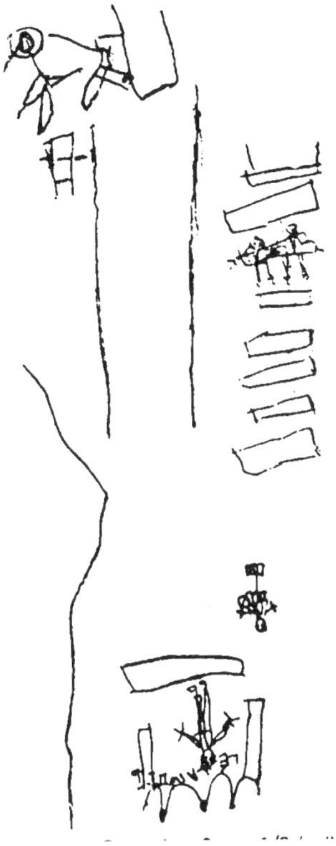

Fig. 68. Simonne Luquet, French, 6;6 (Luquet collection). Concert. Realistic colouring (§50). Rabattement (§76). Mixture of points of view in the chair in the upper left-hand corner (§77).

the child thought worth colouring (fig. 75). The available literature does not allow me to make any firm conclusions about military uniforms. In an extensive collection of the drawings by a French boy produced from six to seven years during the (First World) War, the uniforms of the different forces of the French army and those of the allies or enemies were consistently realistically coloured, at least in their intention. However, in other isolated drawings by various children the uniforms are decoratively coloured just like the clothes of civilians. It has not been possible for me to ascertain whether most children have a distinct preference for one or other of these kinds of colouring, or whether they simply switch from one to the other at will.

Fig. 69. Simonne Luquet, French, 8;2 (Luquet collection). Bird. Decorative colouring of animals (§50).

Fig. 70. Italian girl, 2;6 (after Lombardo-Radice). Bird. Interpretation of an unpremeditated trace (§61). Addition of details improving the resemblance (§62).

Fig. 71. Simonne Luquet, French, 8;6 (Luquet collection). Swan. Decorative colouring of animals (§50).

The deliberate, if no doubt unconscious, nature of these two distinct kinds of colouring and how they are applied to definite classes of objects is especially clear in those drawings where both occur together. One such drawing (fig. 74) combines decorative colouring for the boat and realistic colouring for the sky and the flag. In the drawing of 'a lake' (fig. 76), although the trees are green, the water-lilies are given green leaves and yellow flowers, and the flag of the boat is in tricolour, but the children are clothed in red, yellow and blue, and the ducks each have a different colour: violet, yellow, red and blue. In the drawing of 'a river' (fig. 77), the water and the sky are blue, the trees are green, the parapet of the bridge is violet, and its platform is red, just like the dress of the woman who is crossing over it. The five fish are each drawn in a different colour: maroon, blue, violet, brown, and red. In the drawing of a piano (fig. 65), the girl's signature is decoratively coloured, but the keys of the piano are realistically coloured in black and yellow. Various drawings of men, which have the clothes coloured decoratively, indicate the cheeks by a trace of red (fig. 63). Finally, there is the striking example of a drawing showing a woman returning with the shopping

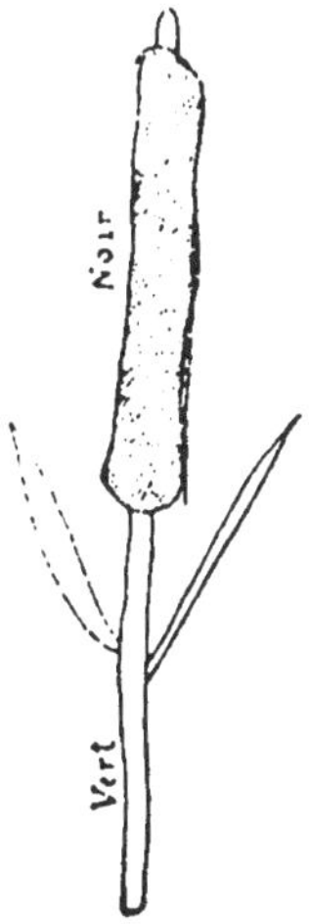

Fig. 72. Simonne Luquet, French, 7 years (Luquet collection). Reed. Realistic colouring of vegetation (§50).

Fig. 73. Simonne Luquet, French, 5 years (Luquet collection). House with garden. Juxtaposition (§68) and changing point of view (§77). Layering of the trees (§73).

Fig. 74. Simonne Luquet, French, 7;3 (Luquet collection). Boat. Mixture of realistic and decorative colouring (§50).

Fig. 75. Simonne Luquet, French, 5;4 (Luquet collection). Church. Addition of a detail through synthesis (§43). Black and white drawing, except for the flag with realistic colouring but where the spatial relation of the colours is inaccurate (§68).

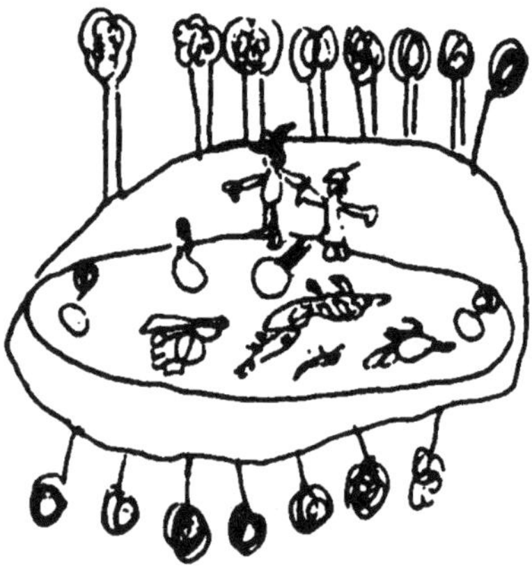

Fig. 76. Simonne Luquet, French, 7;3 (Luquet collection). Lake. Mixture of realistic and decorative colouring (§50). Rabattement (§76).

(fig. 78). Although the colouring of the clothes is purely decorative, the objects she is bringing back in her basket are realistically coloured: two green leeks, a piece of red meat, four red apples, four brown potatoes, two yellow oranges, and a carrot with green leaves.

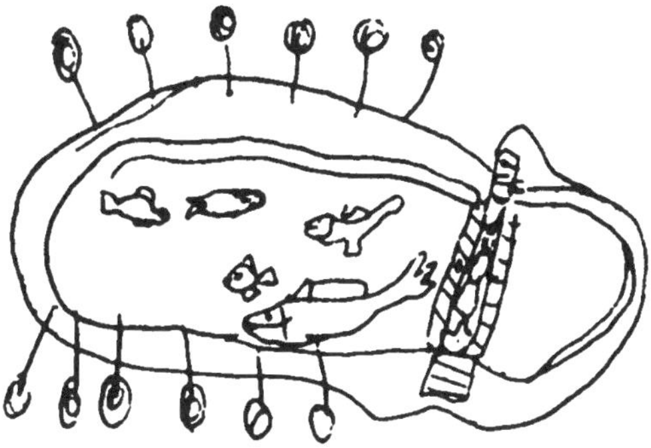

Fig. 77. Simonne Luquet, French, 7;3 (Luquet collection). River. Mixture of realistic and decorative colouring (§50). Rabattement (§76).

Fig. 78. Simonne Luquet, French, 7;3 (Luquet collection). Woman returning with her shopping. Mixture of realistic and decorative colouring (§50). Transparency (§74).

Despite the limited information available, the conclusions they suggest do seem to have some general validity. Indeed, the characteristics of colouring which we have been considering can also be found in comics,[13] and their widespread attraction for children suggests that they closely accord with children's own tendencies.

13. *'images d'Epinal'*

PART 2

THE DEVELOPMENT OF CHILDREN'S DRAWINGS

6
Realism

51. Nothing describes children's drawing in general better than the term realism. Children are realists first of all in their motifs, in the subjects they draw. A drawing consists of a system of lines that through their relation to one another take on a form. But, depending on the intention of the artist, this form can have two different goals. It can be produced either to please the eye simply for its visual appearance, or else to reproduce real objects. It can be, to use the language of the school of Froebel, a 'form of beauty' or a 'form from life'. In simpler terms, there are two kinds of drawing: figurative drawings and non-figurative or, in a broad sense, geometrical drawings.

This second conception of drawing seems to be alien to children. It is not that they are completely insensitive to what one could call abstract beauty, or in particular the pattern of a drawing. For example, a girl (3;8) paused while drawing a man to admire the head which she had just drawn: 'That round shape is beautiful.' But this is just an incidental detail. Even in the unusual circumstances where the child pays it some attention, it is not premeditated, and the essential point of the drawing is to represent something. The idea that a drawing might not represent anything is so strange to children that even when they have drawn something to which they cannot give an exact interpretation they nevertheless claim that it represents 'something'. And since children spontaneously devote themselves to figurative drawings, any attempt to interest them in geometrical drawings proves fruitless. Kindergarten teachers are in complete agreement that the taste of their little students is infinitely less for 'forms of beauty' than for 'forms from life'. I have observed that when children draw a geometrical figure, generally in imitation of other people's drawings, they quickly try to find some figural interpretation and only reproduce the drawing with this interpretation. Thus a three-year-old Californian girl, having drawn some circles, in imitation of some that had been drawn for her, called them cakes and bees. Letters 'H' became ladders. Another child, at four years drew the only geometrical drawing he had ever been seen to produce, a rectangle divided into squares with their diagonals, probably in imitation of a kind of hop-scotch game. When he was asked what it was, he first replied 'Some straight lines', but then added 'But it is a lion's cage'; he then drew the same figure several more times, but always as a cage.

52. Children are not only realist in their choice of motif, but also in its rendition. It might seem *a priori* that a figurative drawing could be nothing other than realistic, since it consists in the graphic translation of the visual characteristics of the represented object. But such a conclusion would be somewhat premature. This translation is not necessarily literal. Its faithfulness depends not solely upon how well it was drawn because of the ability of the artist, but also upon the underlying intention. One recalls the well crafted but inaccurate literary translations of the seventeenth century (known as *'les belles infidèles'*). In art itself, the opposition between the realist and idealist tendencies is very familiar, and appears in the most elementary texts on aesthetics. Thus the issue of whether children are essentially and deliberately realists is not a foregone conclusion, but one to be settled by the facts.

This realist intention could be established first of all by a simple investigation of the form of children's drawings. Close analysis of the drawings, clarified by the verbal explanations given by children, confirms that they do wish to produce an exact representation of the objects they depict, and to reproduce everything that has struck them even if an adult may often completely fail to notice such details. I have selected the following example, not because it is any more realistic than many others, but because in its own way it deals with a theme taken up by professional artists. It is a veritable *'tableau'*, and the young girl (5;9) when explaining the finished drawing gave it the title 'the morning' (fig. 79). It faithfully reproduces what she could see every morning outside her door. Along the road, she has shown the pavement with its trees and gas lamps, and three houses. At the upper windows of each of the houses, the maids are looking out into the road. The doors of the houses are open (indeed, opened outwards), and in front of the two on the right, the maids are cleaning the carpets by hitting them against the trees. The maid of the house on the left is beside the pavement, where she has gone to fetch the milk. In front of her, in the road, there is the milk cart and in the cart the jugs of milk. In the

Fig. 79. Simonne Luquet, French, 5;9 (Luquet collection). Morning. Example of realism (§52).

top right-hand corner there is the house of the milkman and to its left a field with two cows and a chicken.

The most diverse drawings bear witness to children's keen observation, in the number if not the accuracy of the details included in their drawings. So it is unfair to dismiss their drawings as 'monotonous replications of a stereotypic type'. For example, a dog will be given a collar with a tax disc and bells; the child will try to capture the movement of trotting horses, or ducks and swans swimming; people will be individualised by some distinctive characteristic, such as the spectacles of grandmother, the freckles of the maid, or by something unusual about their clothing. Sometimes it is by some physiognomic trait; for example, a young girl (7;3) included teeth in her portrait of her teacher, 'because she is always showing her teeth'. Gestures, such as the most expressive gestures of the arms, are often represented extremely imperfectly and sometimes in an anatomically impossible way. But what matters to us is not the outcome but the child's explicitly stated intention: a soldier saluting, a child thumbing its nose, people showing emotion with their arms wide open or raised up to the skies, as in a drawing where the mother is looking at her daughter who has just dropped a cup of milk on the floor (fig. 80).

The realist tendency of children is especially striking when it triumphs over the general tendency children have to represent the

Fig. 80. Simonne Luquet, French, 7;4 (Luquet collection).
A mother and her daughter who has dropped her cup of milk. Realistic representation of gesture (§52).

details of objects according to their importance for them (§46). This can lead them to represent details they fail to understand, precisely because they do not understand them. Thus, in the drawing of a steam train, a young girl (5;2) drew the dome-shaped structure next to the chimney with its smoke; she did not know what it was for but remarked that 'locomotives have those'. This also explains why many children, even though they leave out a host of other details in their drawings of people, take care to include the navel (fig. 142).

53. In order to bring out the realist intention of children's drawings, I shall no longer concentrate on the drawings themselves since that would require detailed analysis which, to be convincing, could well become tiresome. In any case, children's realist intentions are often obscured by faulty production. In order to ascertain their realistic intention it is both more appropriate and more reliable to make reference, not to the appearance of the drawings, but to the accounts which children give of them. As we have already seen, these accounts demonstrate the seriousness with which the drawings are produced (§3), but, in addition, they also allow us to understand those qualities which, according to the child, ought to be possessed by a drawing whether or not that drawing actually has them. Now, the child's remarks establish conclusively that, as far as he or she is concerned, the essential requirement of a drawing is that it should show some resemblance, either in its overall appearance, or in the number and precision of its details. Thus, a drawing of a man by a girl (3;9) (fig. 22) gave rise to this appreciation: 'It is good: it is such an elegant man' (i.e. like a real man). She then added the ears and found that one, attached to the outline of the face, was good, but the other, which cut through the same outline, was not. At 4;3; having drawn a house, she took hold of it and went triumphantly to show it to her mother, repeating six times over: 'it has everything' (i.e., my drawing includes every detail of a real house). The next day, she drew a man and noted that the hands were good, with their fingers. At 6;9, she drew three pictures of a vase of flowers from life, and wrote under her signature 'the third one is the most beautiful' (i.e. the one with greatest resemblance) because unlike the others it included the square base of the vase (figs 81–83). Regarding a swan she drew when she was eight-and-a-half, she commented that the tail and the open wings were a good resemblance, as was the leg stretched out swimming, but she thought that this leg was also too long, and the neck too short. These comments, taken from just one child, show how realism dominated the whole range of her graphic work.

Figs 81–83. Simonne Luquet, French, 6;9 (Luquet collection). Vase of flowers. Three consecutive drawings. Role of the internal model in drawings from nature (§35). Realism (§53).

Fig. 84. The vase drawn in figures 81–83, based on a photograph.

54. In general, children's concern for realism causes them little trouble. The very idea of seeking a resemblance is sufficient for them to suppose that they must have achieved it, even though an impartial observer might think otherwise. Their ready acceptance of their own creations is also encouraged by their highly developed skill in discovering far-fetched resemblances in their drawings which escape anyone else, as is the case for the unpremeditated drawings (§59). They can nevertheless be dissatisfied with the results, in which

case they check what they have done against reality in order to recognise and correct the imperfections. A seven-year-old Belgian girl, who loved horses and constantly drew them, was never satisfied with her drawings, and incessantly observed every horse she came across, stopping her nurse to look at them. A Californian boy, from the age of 3;10 to 4;1, compared his man drawings with his own body. Once, having drawn one where an arm extended to the ground, he let his arms drop and looked at them to check how long they were. He then said 'Arms are not like that; they do not hang down to the feet.' A Californian girl (2;4), having copied the hands from a drawing by another young girl, looked at her own hands; she seemed unhappy with her work and quickly moved on to another drawing.

55. If children's drawings are essentially realist, then it follows that there should be little evidence of two tendencies opposed to realism: schematism and idealism. And this indeed is the case. By schematism, I do not mean the simplification of the represented object through a reduction in the number of reproduced details and the sketchy representation of those details that are shown. It is true that a number of children's drawings show such characteristics, but, in my view, various authors have been wrong to conclude that this is deliberate schematism. We should first note that, despite the care they usually take in their drawings, children can nevertheless mess them up for a variety of reasons, and they sometimes themselves will describe them as 'hastily done'.

Although one comes across such careless drawings among those children who draw to please themselves, they are naturally much more frequent among the drawings done in class, and it is these drawings from which studies of children's drawings often take most of their examples. These school exercises, so-called 'free drawings', do not hold the same attraction for children as their own entirely spontaneous drawings, where they necessarily take care over how they are produced. In the case of spontaneous and carefully executed drawings, those which in their overall form have a schematic character decrease proportionately with age. In my view, schematism is not characteristic of children's drawings in general, but only of a limited period. In chapter 8, I will argue that what appears to be schematism is really a question of failed realism, constrained by both motor and truly psychological factors, and that realism gradually triumphs as these other factors diminish.

56. Like schematism, idealism plays a very marginal role in children's drawings. It is indeed true that children draw imagined and even imaginary objects, such as tropical countries they have never seen, or scenes from legends or from stories of their own invention, yet such drawings are realist in the sense that they try to represent the actual characteristics of these fictional objects. In contrast, idealism consists in bestowing upon objects characteristics that are alien to the object being represented, with a view to making nature more beautiful than it really is, either by adding additional features to the drawing, or by modifying the shapes corresponding to the real elements (fig. 29), or even by employing what we have called decorative colouring.

I cannot pretend that such idealism is completely alien to children's drawings, since I have come across clear examples in the drawings by my own daughter. For example, when she was six, she drew a train but replaced the single lantern at the front of the locomotive by several of them, and also coloured them red 'since that makes them very pretty'. But as I have not found any mention of anything similar in reports by the most attentive observers of children's drawings, I shall desist from generalising from this single subject since she might be exceptional in this respect. In any case, even for this child, idealism was evident in only relatively few drawings, and they were linked to realism by continuous transitions. Those traces regarded as simple embellishments of the drawing were derived from actual ornaments of the object represented, sometimes because she had forgotten their original meaning (§25), and sometimes because of the confusion which occurs relatively frequently in children between the representation of an object and the object itself (§16). To summarise, according to the present state of the literature, it is very unlikely that more searching observations will fundamentally challenge the conclusion that idealism or schematism have no more than a minor place in children's drawings as a whole. Ultimately, realism is their essential characteristic.

7
First Stage: Fortuitous Realism

57. Children's drawings do not remain the same from beginning to end. So what, then, are the distinctive characteristics of the successive stages?[14] Since, as I have claimed, children's drawings are throughout essentially realistic, it follows that each of these later stages must be distinguished by its own special kind of realism.

A drawing is a combination of lines drawn to represent an actual object, whether or not the intended resemblance is actually achieved. This conception of a drawing is not peculiar to adults. Children as young as three share this same conception, and development involves the overcoming of the obstacles which oppose the expression of this realistic tendency. But although this conception of the drawing arises spontaneously, it is something they acquire by themselves. It is not innate.[15] This conception is preceded by a different one, and I will now consider what this alternative conception involves, how children arrive at it, why they maintain it for a certain period, and then the processes by which it gives way to the conception of drawing in the strict sense.

Children do not initially regard their drawings as a way of making an image, but simply as a means of making marks on paper. To engage in trace making is to execute movements of the hand which, with the aid of various materials, leave behind visible traces on a support such as a sheet of paper. Children can themselves arrive at this idea of a trace and at the intention of producing one. Such movements of the hand are not like those made in response to a task. To begin with, they are the simple effect of the spontaneous release of excess neuromuscular energy, and since they are accompanied by pleasant feelings, the child is stimulated to repeat them. In addition, children touch everything. While they are handling various objects, and aimlessly running their hands over any light surface, they can

14. *'phases'*
15. *'primitive'*

leave traces behind. They can do this even without the aid of another object, since their rather grubby hands will do just as well. Having once produced such traces, children are able to see them, and determine that they were the creator. This unwitting masterpiece may seem to an adult insignificant, if not a nuisance, but for children it is the outcome of their own activity, an expression of their personality, and something they themselves have created. Children are impressed by this discovery of their own creative power. It is a source of a pleasure which they try to renew by making those traces again, though now intentionally where first they were fortuitous. One can see marks on the walls in the streets made with a pencil, chalk, charcoal, or clay, scratches done with a nail or some flint, the automatic affirmations of the presence of their author, or a kind of instinctive signature. When a Californian boy was given a pencil and paper, towards the end of his third year, he sometimes used the pencil to make marks but mainly preferred to make holes in the paper with the point of the pencil.

58. Children who are entirely isolated could thus, all by themselves, develop the intention to make traces. But in fact in most cases, children are led to do so by imitating adults. They see their parents or other adults drawing, writing, or in one way or another making marks by some manual activity, and, noting this activity among other people, they try to imitate them. It goes without saying that children imitate, but why do they imitate? To talk of an 'instinct to imitate' is just to provide a name, not an explanation. First of all, when children imitate what an adult is doing, the aim of that activity is often unclear to them, and may be one that could have no utility for them. They imitate not in order to achieve what another person has done, but to imitate the manner in which he is doing it. For children, imitation is not a means but an end. How, then, does it arise? After all, the wish to imitate does not in itself ensure success. The sight of some movement performed by someone else gives no indication to the observer how they should produce the same movement, and it is only in quite exceptional cases that this is achieved from the outset. Every failed attempt by children at imitation is for them a proof of their inferiority, whereas when they attain success they feel equal to the person they have imitated. As we see it, imitation is a kind of competitive sport for children: it is a chance for them to prove to others and themselves that they are as 'capable' as anyone else.

In summary, children begin to make traces because in producing them they secure clear confirmation of the gift of a power of creativity equal to that of adults.

59. This raises a new problem. At that time in their lives when they are taking pleasure in making lines devoid of any meaning, children have not only seen but also attended to images in books, magazines, and catalogues, and have recognised what is represented, at least in the simplest of such images. They know that traces can resemble something else. Furthermore, many children will have certainly seen someone else drawing, and sometimes will even have seen someone drawing something for them. Sometimes they may have asked for a drawing to be done for them, and will then have seen an adult produce a reasonable likeness of what they themselves asked for, such as a man. Therefore, some children, at least, will have discovered that adults have the power to produce not just mere traces, but rather drawings in the strict sense. Therefore, the tendency to imitate should not be limited, as we have seen, to making traces, but to producing drawings. Yet, even those children who have seen other people make drawings continue for some time to produce mere lines with no figurative intent.

The reason that children initially restrict themselves to trace making is that, during this period, although they are well aware of the graphic faculty in others, they do not believe that they could possess it themselves. When you think about it, it must seem almost like a miracle to children to be able to produce an image of an object – or, as the child sees it, something almost real – just by moving a pencil around on a piece of paper. It is hardly surprising, therefore, that children should begin by supposing they cannot do it, and that it is something special to adults. It is possible they do not even dream of imitating adults in this way, since they are convinced that such attempts would be doomed to failure. In fact, I have never come across an example of any children trying to represent something in their drawings during this period. Those children encouraged to risk making the attempt by the invitations and encouragement of those around them are eventually compelled through this experience to admit their helplessness. An American psychologist (J.M. Baldwin) repeatedly asked his daughter, during the last six months of her second year, and the first three months of her third, to do some proper drawings for him: 'there was on her face an expression of dissatisfaction with her later attempts, similar to that which one observes in the efforts of the year-old to speak.

My little girl would hide her head after making a drawing, extend the pencil to me, and say, "Papa, make man." It seemed to indicate a sense of what was expected beyond the ability to attain the process of accomplishing it.'[16]

60. However, the day comes when children notice a more or less vague resemblance between one of their traces and some actual object. They then regard the trace as a representation of that object, and to prove it they announce the interpretation they have given it: a mouse by a Californian girl (2;5), an umbrella by a Dutch girl of the same age, a bird by an Italian girl (2;6) (fig. 70), a windmill by a French boy (3;3), and 'a big dog with his big tail' by a Belgian boy (3;6).

According to direct observations of several children, corroborated by the evidence provided from adults about their own childhood memories, children, when they first discover that they have produced an image are filled with intense joy, reminiscent of the famous words: 'I too am a painter' – *Anch'io son pittore.*[17]

But the joy does not last. Since the resemblance was produced fortuitously, this happy coincidence will not immediately occur again, and children are then forced to recognise that it was only by accident that they managed to produce a resemblance. They thus continue for some time to make traces that are neither followed by a figurative interpretation nor provoked by any representative intention (32).

Nevertheless, accidental resemblances continue to occur from time to time in their drawings, and children notice them even more often once they are expecting them to appear by chance, or by 'a kind of magic' as one psychologist, recalling his own memories of childhood, has put it. In this way, children come to appreciate that their traces can, not just under exceptional circumstances, but as a matter of course, resemble something else.

61. Thus children are led to give interpretations to each of their own traces. This is determined by the same general factors discussed already in chapter 2: the resemblance of the whole drawing or a certain detail to something else, and also external circumstances. But

16. J.M. Baldwin, (1895). *Mental development in the child and the race*. New York: Macmillan, p. 84.
17. These words are attributed to the Italian painter, Antonio Allegri da Correggio (1494–1534) awed at the sight of Raphael's 'St Cecilia' in Bologna, in 1525. As Michele Sinico and Giulia Parovel have pointed out to me, these words were not boastful, but an expression of humility.

these interpretations are very unstable, for two related reasons. On the one hand, the interpretation is not supported, as it will later be, by the memory of the intention, since the traces were not produced with any representative intent. On the other hand, since the shape of these traces hardly resembles one thing any more than another, the child, resolute on finding a meaning, is able to see the representation of almost anything in their drawing. Since the interpretation the child applies to the traces corresponds to whatever object the child happens to have in mind at the time, the same traces may often receive several quite different interpretations in succession. For example, for some Belgian children aged from three years to three-and-a-half, a dog and then 'some evil men', a see-saw and then a bed; balloons and then fish in a canal; 'many soldiers' and then sheep in the field; for a French girl (3;8), a table and then an aeroplane.

62. At this time, children still lack full possession of the graphic faculty. Although they are now quite capable of producing in a consistent rather than just sporadic way traces that, at least to their eyes, resemble something, none of their drawings has yet been preceded or provoked by the intention to depict a particular object. The transition from the production of involuntary to premeditated images occurs through the intermediary of drawings that are in part involuntary and part deliberate.

The fortuitous resemblance between the trace and the object named by the child is rather crude, and the child, whilst noting the resemblance is well aware of its imperfection, and thus naturally tries to produce a better resemblance. An English boy (2;6), having 'with a rapture of joy' recognised smoke in a spiral line he had drawn, hastened to add some more. An Italian girl (2;6), who had seen a bird in one of her traces, added two vertical lines for the legs (fig. 70). A three-year-old Belgian girl completed one of her traces that she had interpreted as a cage with a dot depicting the sparrow it contained. A French girl of three-and-a-half, having interpreted one of her traces as a bird, added the beak, the eye, and the legs, and six weeks later when she saw a bear in one of her drawings she completed it with an eye.

Although, in such cases, the accentuation of the resemblance is limited to very simple additions, the result is generally satisfying. Children can thus rightly be claimed to have the ability to improve a fortuitous resemblance intentionally. They repeat such improvements more and more intentionally with practice, and the success of their repeated attempts strengthens their awareness of this ability.

63. Two steps are involved, therefore, when a fortuitous resemblance is intentionally perfected. The second step, the production of the complementary resemblance, is intentional, such as the deliberate addition of the legs to something the child has judged to look like an animal. But the first step, the production of the initial resemblance, is unintentional. Consequently, the drawing as a whole cannot be regarded as a drawing in the strict sense, i.e. one caused by a prior intention to produce an image not merely of any object but something in particular. The child cannot therefore strictly be credited with a fully developed graphic faculty. Yet, since the initial resemblance, although unwitting, is no less the child's work than the planned complementary resemblance, the child might imagine that he must be capable of deliberately producing the former as well as the latter, or at least wonder if it is worth trying. The attempt might or might not succeed, but the child could not succeed at all without being tempted to try, and the child would not try at all if he did not think that success was possible.

Furthermore, the circumstances favour the success of the child's attempt. As a result of the tendency towards immediate graphic automatism (§12), when children attempt to produce a deliberate likeness, this usually is an attempt to depict something they have just represented fortuitously. This is what happened on two occasions separated by ten days in the case of a boy (3;8), who, having drawn a curved line which he then interpreted as a croquet hoop, immediately drew a croquet hoop on purpose. Since there was no delay between the production of the fortuitous and deliberate resemblances, the conditions under which the two drawings were produced were as similar as possible, and hence the drawings themselves were also nearly the same. Furthermore, as we have already noted, the subjective sense of resemblance is only partly determined by the actual level of similarity; the memory of the intention can be sufficient to convince the child that the drawing is a good likeness.

From that moment, the child's traces bring together all the elements of a drawing in the strict sense of the word: the intention, its execution, and the interpretation corresponding to the intention. However crude their productions, children have, from this point, completely acquired the graphic faculty. In this respect, they have become equal to their elders, and they are proud of this. A young boy (3;10), on showing off his second deliberate drawing, proudly declared: 'now I have become a drawer just like Simonne [his sister]'.

Aware of their graphic faculty, children willingly put it into practice, and from that moment on they will often announce beforehand what they are going to draw. The initial stage, prior to drawing in the strict sense, has thereby come to a close.

Needless to say, the account I have given is necessarily rather schematic. Although I have tried to stress the continuity between the different phases of this development, they are really less distinct than my analysis might nevertheless seem to suggest. The onset and duration of each of these phases varies considerably from one child to another. In particular, in the case of a girl (4;1) I was able to observe this preliminary stage in its entirety, from the first traces devoid of representational intent to the first intentional drawing, announced before it was produced. The whole process took no more than a quarter of an hour. But even in this extraordinarily rapid example of development, no doubt caused by the relatively advanced age of this child, the different phases were clearly recognisable, and their succession and the psychological basis for the transition from each one to the next conformed with the analysis I have been presenting.

I should also stress that not only does each stage of development emerge out of the preceding one through an almost indiscernible progression, but the former stages extend for a rather long time into the following ones, and only gradually diminish. Thus the acquisition of each stage is by no means immediately decisive. For example, children who have already applied interpretations to their fortuitous traces and deliberately improved their resemblance will still continue to produce traces that, once completed, are given no meaning at all.

Furthermore, even when the stage of premeditated drawings has begun, the child does not only produce intentional drawings but also drawings that have not been provoked by any representational intention. Even when they are finished, they are still treated as meaningless traces.

In short, children begin by making traces simply for the sake of making marks. Although they know that traces drawn by other people can represent a particular object and do so effectively, they do not entertain the same possibility for their own traces. It is only later that they come to draw with the intention of representing something, once they have found that their traces have accidentally produced a resemblance that they themselves had not tried to make. This first phase of children's drawings, fortuitous realism, becomes transformed into intentional realism by a continuous series of transitions.

8
Second Stage: Failed Realism

64. Once having progressed to drawing in the proper sense, children want to be realists. But such intentions are initially hindered by obstacles preventing them from being realised. I will call this stage *failed realism*.

The first obstacle confronting their attempts at realism is of a purely physical nature: children at this stage still do not know how to control and constrain their graphic movements so as to produce the desired appearance. They are like novice violinists constantly hitting wrong notes. This awkwardness in execution, which does gradually decrease, means that at least some of the earliest drawings are totally incomprehensible even with the help of explanations from the child. I will restrict myself to one very clear example because of its simplicity. On several occasions, the child tried to draw a rectangle to depict, for example, the side view of a house (often forgetting to include the roof at first), the front of a house, a plan view of a house, a room of the house, a door, a window, a bed, and so on. In fact, the rectangle was often drawn in the most varied ways: sometimes as a closed contour with a roughly circular or elliptical shape; sometimes as an incomplete outline open on two or three sides; and sometimes as a triangle. Even in the case of a girl of four years and three months, shapes she meant to be rectangular turned out as triangles.

But it is not the case that the child simply wants to draw an outline and does not care about its precise shape. The same girl when she was three-and-a-half, having drawn eight outlines of houses with diverse and inexact shapes, explained what she was trying to do by means of the following gestures: 'A big line like that: ⇒, and then a line like that: ⇓, and then a line like that: ⇓; and then a big line like that: ⇒' (i.e. a rectangle wider than it was high).

65. The realist intention encounters yet another obstacle though not of a graphic but truly psychological nature: the limited and discontinuous character of the child's attention.

This explains why children in their initial drawings include a very limited number of the details or actual elements of the object represented. They certainly know about the details they leave out of their drawings, for these are just as visible as the ones they include, and, what is more, when they are describing the actual object, sometimes even while they are drawing it, they often refer to details they do not draw. Nor is it the case that, although fully aware of the existence of those details, they never bother to depict them, since, in fact, drawings of the same motif produced soon or even immediately after one another may sometimes include a detail and sometimes leave it out. In fact, children have the intention to represent all those details they are thinking about. To be more precise, to the extent that they are thinking about them, their mental representations are expressed in their graphic movements. As we have seen (§44), children think of the details of an object in a certain order corresponding to the degree of importance they attribute to them, and they will continue to add them as long as their attention moves from those details which have already been drawn to a new one. But their attention can rapidly wander, since they are faced with a double task: on the one hand, the task of thinking about the object that needs to be represented, and, on the other, the task of monitoring the graphic movements to produce this representation. Once the child's attention wanders, however, the drawing is regarded as finished, however incomplete it may seem to an adult. For example, a boy (3;6) drew a man without a mouth or a nose, and when asked 'Is that all?' he replied 'It's finished.' And yet just before he had included those details in another man drawing. Furthermore, having finished this drawing, he added those details to a man drawing he had earlier drawn on the same sheet of paper but which had previously lacked those details (figs 85–87). Similarly, an American girl (4;8) drew a man as follows: the outline of the head, the eyes, the arms, the legs and feet, and buttons between the legs. She then added hands at the end of each arm, and then stopped, regarding her drawing as now finished. When her mother asked her if the eyes were the only details of the head, she added the mouth, a beard, the nose, hair, and ears, thus demonstrating that the reason she had not previously included them was simply that her attention had strayed having drawn the other details according to their order of importance.

66. Until now I have been considering details missing from the drawing even though they occur in the object it is meant to

Figs 85–87. Constant M., French, 3;6 (Luquet collection). Men. Three immediately consecutive drawings. Men without trunk and with their arms attached to their heads (§23) (with a hint of a trunk in the first). The nose and the mouth, which were initially absent in the first, were only added after the second drawing. These details are also missing from the third drawing (§65). In the first drawing, the mouth is drawn above the nose (§68).

represent. I now turn to those details that are in fact included in the drawing. The defects that occur can be explained by the fact that when children are thinking about depicting any particular detail, they think solely about how they are going to add it to their drawing. Hypnotised by this detail, they forget about the other details they have already drawn, and they do not see them even though they are in front of their eyes. When they visually perceive the object itself, they apprehend at once the combination of elements and their inter-relationships. But in the successive and discontinuous representation which they have of these elements while they are being drawn, these relations escape them. They know about them, but they do not think about them. When looking at the finished drawing, adults perceive the entire drawing in terms of how the details relate to one another, and they are thus led to suppose that these relations are faulty, when, in fact, for the child, there is just an absence of relations.

67. This general imperfection of the drawing, which is the essential characteristic of the stage of failed realism and which I call synthetic incapacity, occurs for a range of relations, above all, for proportions. In a number of drawings, the relative dimensions of various elements bear no correspondence to their actual counterparts. For example, man drawings by various children show the hair as longer than the legs. These disproportions can occur for several reasons, such as lack of skill, or the inability to stop the trace at the desired moment. In other cases, the available space on the paper can lead to the shortening of certain traces through lack of

space, or, conversely, to the lengthening of others through 'horror of a vacuum'. Often, the exaggeration of the dimensions of a detail can also arise from an unconscious expression of its importance for the child. Sometimes, the importance of an element is determined by the subject of the drawing, as in drawings of ball games or snowball fights, where the active arm is not just shown without the other, but is also extremely elongated (fig. 55). A completely characteristic example comes from a drawing by a Belgian boy (4;4), representing three boys grinding coffee (fig. 88), where the coffee mills, as the centre of interest, are at least as big as the people using them. When a new detail is introduced to the drawing of a particular subject, its size is often exaggerated reflecting the interest of this new detail for the child. But the main reason for the lack of proportions between the traces in a drawing is that each of them is drawn with reference solely to itself, since while it is being drawn, the child gives no thought to the traces drawn before. For example, a girl (3;6) declared two days in a row that a house is represented by a rectangle which is wider than it is high, and yet although her first drawing conformed to the description, the second showed a rectangle which was higher than it was wide.

Fig. 88. Maurice, Belgian, 4;4 (after Rouma). Three children turning a coffee-mill. Neglect of proportions (§67).

Fig. 89. Bavarian girl, 7 years (after Kerschensteiner). Horse-rider. Multiplication of legs (§32). Changing point of view (§§47 and 77). Horse-rider without arms (§68).

68. This neglect of the relations between the different elements of an object is especially clear in relations involving position, which are often falsely depicted. For example, elements which are really connected are depicted as separate, as in the case of a girl (3;4) who announced that she was going to draw a horse. She first drew four vertical lines as the legs, and then announced that she was going to do the head which she tried, unsuccessfully, to draw on the other

end of the sheet of paper. In several of her drawings of churches, until she was four years and two months, the tower and the nave were drawn some distance apart. Until she was five-and-a-half, similar separations occurred for houses and their attached gardens (fig. 73) and also for rooms shown in plan view (fig. 52) in drawings of houses along a road. Several observers have noted how many children will, at first, set out the different parts of their man drawings at some distance from one another (fig. 54). Later, an object held by a person may be merely drawn beside him, even when he has arms, such as an umbrella beside the body, or a pipe outside of the mouth. Often one sees chimneys floating above houses (fig. 17), horse-riders above their horses (fig. 90), and hats above the head (figs 24–26, 92, 130).

Fig. 90. Jean Luquet, French, 5 years (Luquet collection). Horse and rider. Man in the air above his horse (§68).

Fig. 91. Victor, Belgian, 3;6 (after Rouma). Man drawing. Buttons of the clothes above the head (§68). Potatoes in the belly, even though the belly is not depicted.

Sometimes, it is not just the relation of contact that is subject to such separation but also the relation of inclusion. Occasionally, man drawings can show the eyes outside the outline of the face. The buttons of a man's coat were drawn outside of the body by a Belgian boy (4;6), and largely around the head by another boy (3;6) (fig. 91). A Belgian girl (3;6) drew the apples of an apple tree all around the tree; a four-year-old, drawing a portrait of her father, drew the 'frame' beside his father; and a five-year-old girl (who was slightly retarded) drew the door and windows outside the outline of a house. In a series of drawings by a French girl of houses with their rooms shown in plan view, one or other room was drawn outside the overall outline

Fig. 92. Pierre R., French, 5;6 (Luquet Collection). Carnival float. Mixture of intellectual and visual realism: two nostrils but one eye (§79); hat in the air (§68 and 73); rider floating above the horse (§68).

of the house, or the pieces of furniture outside the room to which it belonged; conversely, sometimes even in the same drawings, the courtyard or garden attached to the house was represented inside the house. In general, the edges of adjacent rooms are separated by a space, and this separation between the rooms even persists when the rooms are provided with doors, which are sometimes explicitly claimed to connect those rooms. Consequently, the same door is quite often depicted twice, once for each of the rooms connected by that door. Often the door is attached as best it can to the side of a room, often just opposite the other room which it should have led into. It is already something of a breakthrough when the door connecting two rooms is depicted as a kind of corridor encroaching upon each of the rooms at the same time.

Synthetic incapacity is responsible for the neglect not only of general relations such as contact and inclusion but also more specific relations of location between the elements of the same object. A wide range of children draw the fingers not at the ends of the arms but along their whole length, making the arm look like a leafy branch (figs 23, 27). The tricolour flag shown in a drawing of a church by a girl (5;4) was not divided into three parallel stripes: the red was in the centre, the white on the side opposite the pole, and the blue extended along all three other sides (fig. 75). In the drawings of many children, umbrellas or parasols held closed and downwards, like a cane, are not held by the handle but at the other end. In boat drawings, the rudder can be at the front, and the towing rope is either attached at the rear or on the wrong side of the boat for towing. Houses can have the door between the windows and the chimney, men can have their mouth above their nose (fig. 85) and even their eyes or legs may be attached to the top of the head. One girl (3;6) was quite content to put the tail of a dog in front of its head. A Belgian girl (4;6), in a portrait of her teacher, attached the shoes to the legs at the level of the knees, even though she had already drawn her feet. In the drawings by another child (5;6), supposed to represent people sitting down, the people were shown standing upright superimposed over their chairs with the seats drawn across their faces (fig. 93). In a host of drawings of horse-riders, the spatial relation between rider and horse is depicted in the most varied and sometimes most unexpected ways. The child arrives very slowly at the correct depiction of the person sitting astride the horse, with the first leg occluding the body of the animal and the other leg occluded by the horse. Instead, the two legs are often shown in the same plane, either both in front or else both behind the horse; sometimes they are resting on the ground, as if the person is simply standing beside the horse. In addition to riders floating in the air as it were, above the horse (§47), we find them standing on the horse (figs 92 and 100), without the least intention of depicting a show of horsemanship, and riders may even be drawn inside the body of the horse (fig. 112). Quite often, the rider lacks legs (fig. 89): the depiction of the upper half of the body is judged to be enough to indicate the seated posture.

Fig. 93. Alida, Belgian, 5;6 (after Rouma). Her parents at the table. Neglect of topographic relations (§68).

69. Orientation is a further aspect of the relative positioning of the details within any drawing, and again synthetic incapacity is involved. I am not referring here to children's indifference to the orientation of the entire drawing in relation to the surface on which it is drawn, e.g. paper, blackboard, or a wall, since although this is

very common its psychological interpretation remains obscure. In a number of drawings, certain details are given an orientation quite at odds with the others, and yet the child is not at all perturbed. For example, in two drawings of churches drawn 15 days apart by a three-and-a-half-year-old girl, the tower and the nave were shown head to tail; 12 days later in another church drawing, the walls of the tower and nave were shown at right angles to one another. In drawings by various children, people shown inside a house either have their heads towards the floor, or are horizontal. In many drawings of houses, the tip of the roof is directed not at the sky but towards the ground (figs 17 and 95).

Fig. 94. House. Off-vertical chimney, which is instead perpendicular to the roof (§36).

Fig. 95. House. Roof pointing inwards. (§69).

Fig. 96. 'An egg with a duck inside.' Transparency (§74).

70. So far, I have been examining the principal manifestations of synthetic incapacity. This gradually diminishes to the extent that the child's attention becomes less disconnected and, if I may say so, less desultory. Children are then able when drawing a detail to think at the same time about the other details they have already included in the drawing, and, as a result, to sense and render the relations among them. On examining a collection of drawings by the same child, one can see each of the defects that had occurred in the earlier drawings disappearing over time. But I should also add, as I have done before, progress not only occurs through almost imperceptible gradations, but can even include periods of stagnation or even regression. Synthetic incapacity is not defeated at a single stroke. On the one hand, for any given drawing, synthetic incapacity may be overcome in some respects, but persist in others. For example, in plan views of houses the outlines of some adjacent rooms are shown connected, but others are still separated by a space. On the other

hand, in a series of drawings produced by the same child over time, certain defects that occurred at the beginning disappear for a while but then reappear in later drawings, and it is only after a somewhat lengthy period of such fluctuations that they are finally eliminated.

9
Third Stage: Intellectual Realism

71. Once children have overcome the problem of synthetic incapacity,[18] nothing stands in the way of their drawings being completely realistic, that is to say, depicting both the details of the represented object and their interrelationships. But the realism of the child is in no way that of the adult. Whereas adults are committed to *visual* realism, children are proponents of *intellectual* realism. For adults, any drawing, if it is to provide a resemblance, must be a kind of photograph of the object, reproducing all those details, but only those details, which can be seen from where the object is viewed, and with the shape they form from that viewpoint. In short, the object has to be depicted in perspective. For children, however, a drawing can only be a good likeness if it includes all of the actual details of the object, even if they are not visible either from the location from which they are observed or from any other viewpoint. Instead, they give to each detail its characteristic form, in accord with the principle of exemplarity (§47).

72. Intellectual realism can go so far as to depict in a drawing, not just actual details which are not visible, but even abstract elements which exist only in the mind of the artist. Thus in a drawing of the garden of a house (fig. 97), the paths are indicated by distinct curvy lines, even though they were in fact just the empty spaces between the flower beds. Similarly, the soil in which flowers were planted is represented by a line inside the flower beds, even though there were no such lines in reality.

A similar example comes from a drawing by a Dutch boy (fig. 98) representing a field of potatoes, which displays in the clearest possible way the opposition between intellectual and visual realism. He drew nothing that can actually be seen in a field of potatoes, namely that part of the plants showing above ground, but solely the invisible elements, the tubers under the ground, along with an

18. In other words, the failure to organise the parts of a drawing in relation to one another, either spatially or logically.

Fig. 97. Simonne Luquet, French, 5 years (Luquet collection). House with a courtyard and a garden. Tadpole men with arms attached to their heads (§23). Representation of abstract elements (§72). Mixture of points of view (§77).

element which has no objective existence, but solely an abstract one, the outline of the field.

Similarly, in their drawings of people, various children surround some features of the face with a contour even though those features are not really separate from the rest. This happens for the cheeks, which are sometimes indicated by a dab of red (fig. 63) in coloured drawings or else by a circle (fig. 102), but in this case one might allow that the 'apples' of the cheeks are somewhat set apart by their rosy colouring. But such separation also occurs for the forehead where this explanation no longer applies. A Dutch boy drew a small circle towards the bottom of the trunk in one of his man drawings, which he claimed represented the tummy. Similarly, in drawings of quadrupeds or birds, since children regard the head and body as two

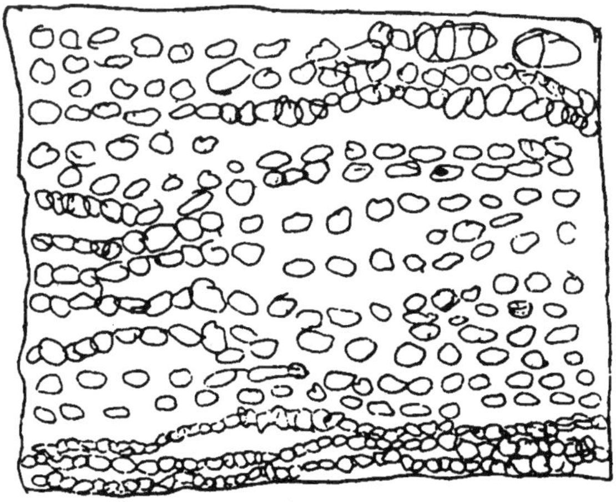

Fig. 98. Dutch boy, 7 years (after Schreuder). Field of potatoes. Intellectual realism (§72).

quite different elements each with its own distinct name, they are often shown by two connected outlines or by a single shape divided in two by a line at the neck (figs 112 and 134), even though in reality they form a single entity with nothing to separate them visually. Two children, an American and a Belgian, are reported to have represented the line of sight by a line joining the eye of the person to the object being looked at.

It is no doubt a similar preoccupation that is responsible for children's use of captions. I cannot accept the explanation which is often given, namely, that children, aware of the imperfection of their own drawings, think that a caption is necessary in order to allow other people to understand what they have tried to represent. As a general rule, children do not draw with a view to a public, but solely for their own personal satisfaction. When they show their 'beautiful' drawings to other people, it is to show off their skill and not to expose their lack of ability by drawing attention to the deficiencies in their drawings. I acknowledge the point of captions in the case of portraits in which the drawing merely shows an anonymous person, but children also add captions to drawings that are perfectly clear to any adults, and hence must be there for the sake of the child. Furthermore, they begin to add captions even before they know how to write. How could they hope to use illegible words to clarify the meaning of drawings they alone can understand? Indeed, children themselves provide the proof that they are fully aware that such captions are unintelligible. At the age when they still do not know how to write with letters, they tend to make themselves understood instead by spontaneously resorting to pictography. This is what happens in 'letters' written to *Père Janvier,* to *petit Noël* or to *Saint Nicholas* by many different children around the age of four to five, in both Europe and America, to ask for Christmas presents. Their letters are, in fact, composed of drawings of the desired objects.

The reason why children add captions to their drawings is no doubt partly because they have seen them attached to diagrams in their school textbooks, and even earlier to their own pictures or perhaps drawings their parents have drawn for them. But this is not the sole nor even primary reason. For children, the name of the object is as essential to the object as its other parts, and therefore has to be included in the drawing. As far as children are concerned, the name of an object is virtually one of its attributes and so inseparable from it that they sometimes experience the need to write it not only on their drawings but even on the actual object, as if it would be incomplete without it.

The same could be said for the signature. Its point is not to reveal the identity of the artist to some third party; rather, the fact that the drawing was produced by such-and-such a person is as much one of the elements of the drawing as the fact that it represents such-and-such an object. Those graffiti accompanied by the signature 'What's my name?' or the inscription 'Signed: Come-and-Get-Me!' demonstrate that children feel that their work should be provided with a signature even when they have no desire to reveal their identity.

73. Intellectual realism gives rise to the use of a variety of techniques, but although some do not go beyond what one might expect of a child of six or seven, others do make one think instead of engineering or architectural drawings. Although these techniques might seem the special province of experts, children not only invent them spontaneously, but can distinguish between them. The way they choose among them on any particular occasion is always determined by the principle of intellectual realism: to present the greatest number, if not all, of the essential elements of the represented object, and to preserve each in its characteristic shape, 'in itself' as it were.

Fig. 99. Bavarian girl, 6 years (after Kerschensteiner). Man. Individual hairs (§73). Frontal view of the eyes in a profile head (§77).

Fig. 100. Bavarian girl, 7 years (after Kerschensteiner). Horse and rider. Hairs on the man and the horse are shown individually (§73). Mixture of viewpoints as a result of the principle of exemplarity of form (§47). Rider 'standing' on the horse (§68).

The simplest of the methods can take various forms but always involves the separation of details in the drawing which in the actual object are not easy to distinguish and may even be obscured by one another. Separations of this kind may be mistaken for mere lack of skill or (in other words) synthetic incapacity (§68). Often the hairs of people and animals are shown individually (figs 23, 99, 100). In a number of man drawings, the hat is shown just touching the top of the head or else floating in the air above it, no doubt, in some cases at least, in order to avoid concealing the forehead. Similarly, trains are represented above the railway track, with the wheels separate from the rails. Furthermore, the wheels on the far side of the train can appear complete beside those on the near side even though they would be partly concealed by them; in addition, the wheels on both sides of the train are shown as complete circles touching the bottom edge of the carriages, even though in reality only their bottom half would be visible (figs 14 and 103). Elements situated in different planes in a scene are set one above the other in tiers so that they are not even partially occluded by those in front of them. This is very evident in drawings containing rows of trees (fig. 56), or couples at a wedding (fig. 56). In various drawings of men where the face is shown frontally, the nostrils are moved from the bottom of the nose to its front (fig. 104) and sometimes even set above one another in order to render them more visible (fig. 105). A drawing of a doll (fig. 64) fails to take account of the fact that although the strings of an apron can be drawn out sideways when it is not being worn, they would not be when worn by the doll, since the apron would not stay on. In a drawing by a boy of six-and-a-half of his father about to pick up his newspaper from a chair, the newspaper is shown floating in the air above the chair (fig. 106).

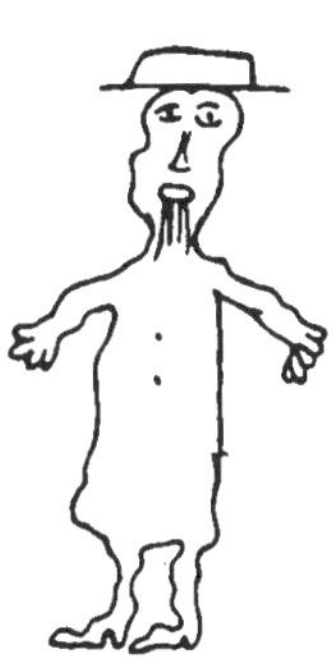

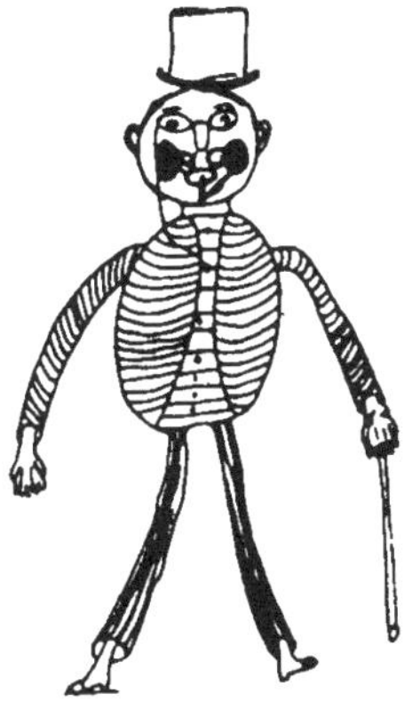

Fig. 101. Bavarian boy, 9 years (after Kerschensteiner). Man. Hat just touching the head (§73). Frontal view of body, but profile view of the feet (§77).

Fig. 102. Bavarian girl, 11 years (after Kerschensteiner). Man. Hat just touching the head (§73). Representation of the cheeks (§72).

Fig. 103. Simonne Luquet, French, 8;8 (Luquet collection). Train. Wheels in the air in relation to the rails and shown in their entirety (§73), without rabattement (§76).

Fig. 104. Jean Luquet, French, 6;10 (Luquet collection). Woman pushing a pram. The top of the head is visible under the hat; tacit correction rather than transparency (§74). Intellectual realism in the depiction of the nostrils (§73). Mixture of viewpoints (§77).

74. Another relatively simple method for showing the invisible elements of an object is known as transparency, and involves depicting details that would otherwise occlude other elements as if they were transparent, thus allowing the other elements to be seen. I will set aside examples which could be more appropriately explained as tacit correction (§4), such as the bodies of people visible under their clothes or under the covers of a bed, toes visible inside shoes, or the top of the head inside a hat (figs 104 and 131). But one encounters a great number of houses where the furniture and the inhabitants are shown as if the front wall of the house were transparent (fig. 108); travellers are visible through the sides of railway carriages; baskets reveal their contents, as in the drawing by a girl (7;8) of a woman returning from shopping (fig. 78); trees show their roots under the ground (fig. 138); plants in pots show the stalk through the earth and the side of the pot (fig. 107); and horse-riders have the leg on the far side of the horse drawn inside the body of the horse, as in a drawing by a girl (6;10) who, while drawing the two legs, explicitly stated that they were on either side of the horse. A four-year-old Belgian boy liked drawing birds laying eggs, and showed the laid eggs under the body of the bird and the other eggs inside its body. Representation of the internal organs is very rare. I

have encountered just one single example, by a boy of 11, in a collection of man drawings by 4000 school boys and girls from Anvers ranging from 3 to 13 years; but this should be attributed, at least for the youngest children, to ignorance of anatomy. A Californian girl of almost three-and-a-half did show the internal organs in her earliest man drawings (fig. 57); in another man drawing done during the same period she drew the partition inside the nose which she expressly stated to be 'what we have between both sides of our nose'. The heart is shown inside the body of a man in drawings by a six-year-old and a seven-your-old from schools in Munich (fig. 109). A five-year-old French boy drew several drawings of 'an egg with a duckling inside' (fig. 96). Another child, at seven, drew a hand (fig. 110), and when asked 'Why are their lines inside the hand?' replied 'They are the nerves.' 'But I have never seen them in my hand' – 'They are inside the flesh.' In a drawing of a 'twelfth night cake', a French girl (3;5) tried to show the lucky charm inside it. Out of 20 Belgian school children asked to draw a funeral procession, 18 drew the body visible on the hearse. One even finds examples of double transparency, where the corpse is visible through the coffin, which in turn is visible inside the hearse, as in the case of a Belgian boy (7;6) and an Irish boy (8 years) from a school in California (fig. 142).

Fig. 105. Simonne Luquet, French, 4;6 (Luquet collection). Lady. Man drawing with no trunk and with his arms attached to his head (§23). Intellectual realism in the representation of the nostrils (§73).

75. A somewhat more complicated technique is the plan, which involves showing the object projected onto the ground surface, as from a bird's eye view. This mode of representation is used for the interiors of houses to show the furniture of the rooms, even though the outsides of the houses are depicted frontally. Although upright pieces of furniture (such as chairs, armchairs, and sofas) are shown

Fig. 106. Jean Luquet, French, 6;6 (Luquet collection). His father about to pick up a newspaper from a chair. The newspaper is in the air (§73).

Fig. 107. Simonne Luquet, French, 6 years (Luquet collection). Yellow marguerite in a flower pot. Transparency of the pot (§74). Depiction of the hole in the bottom of the pot (§77). Realistic colouring of the plant (§50).

from the side (in elevation), to highlight what the child considers to be their characteristic feature, those items of furniture which are not upright (tables, music-stools, stoves) are usually represented in plan view to capture their round or rectangular form.

76. In plan representations, the object is shown from an unusual, but possible, viewpoint. In some cases this viewpoint may perhaps even correspond to an actual perspective, such as items of furniture which are not very tall (bath tubs, piano-stools, *chaises longues*, and low cupboards), or creepy-crawlies like silk-worms, which are usually viewed from above rather than the side. But we encounter an absolutely impossible kind of perspective in the case of a novel technique which I term 'folding out' or 'rabattement', a procedure which is applied from the outset to the supports of objects, such as the feet and legs of animals and furniture and the wheels of vehicles. This involves folding out each of these supports as though they were connected to the object by hinges around which they can be turned.

To some extent, this mode of representation is required by intellectual realism, since it is the only way to show the supports of an object in a bird's eye view that would otherwise be hidden. Hence it is commonly used to depict the feet of beds, tables, and stoves (fig. 52) or the wheels of vehicles (figs 9 and 111). But rabattement no longer has the same *raison-d'être* when objects are drawn in elevation, and as a general rule it is not used for their supports, such as the wheels of railway trains (figs 14 and 103). And yet there are

Fig. 108. Jean Luquet, French, 6;4 (Luquet collection). House. Transparency (§74). Rabattement (§76).

examples from many different children of drawings of animals and less often birds in profile with two rows of legs, one extending from the belly, and the other from the back (fig. 112).

The use of rabattement in plan views of objects is not limited to their supports, but is extended to vertical parts of the object which bear the same kind of relation as the supports except that they point upwards rather than towards the base. For example, in a drawing of a cradle (fig. 113), the main body of the cradle with its netting base is shown in plan, the legs are splayed out on each side, the canopy with its curtains and ribbon knot at the top is folded out at right angles to the legs. Similarly, the hoods of carriages or prams are

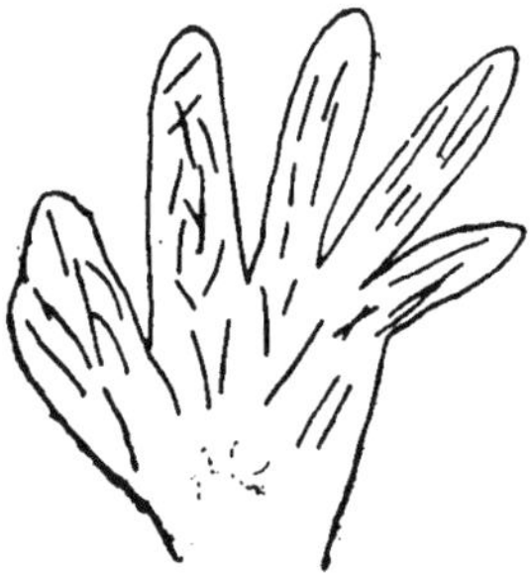

Fig. 109. Bavarian boy, 7 years (after Kerschensteiner). Young girl. Absence of clothes (§46). Arms less advanced than the legs (§46). Displacement of the plait through intellectual realism. Transparency (§74).

Fig. 110. Albert, French, 7 years (Luquet collection). Hand. Transparency (§74).

folded outwards even though in this position they could not fulfil their role, leaving the occupants of the vehicle open to the elements.

Through a still more daring analogy, rabattement is applied to objects standing upright on the ground and having the same kind of

Fig. 111. Simonne Luquet, French, 7;7 (Luquet collection). Horse and carriage. Rabattement of the wheels and the hood of the carriage (§76). Mixture of viewpoints (§77).

relation to the ground as do the headboard and footboard to the mattress of a bed. In its simplest form, this extension of rabattement is used to depict two objects facing one another, where, in essence, there are two planes parallel to one another, and each is perpendicular to the ground. In this case, the objects are folded out onto the

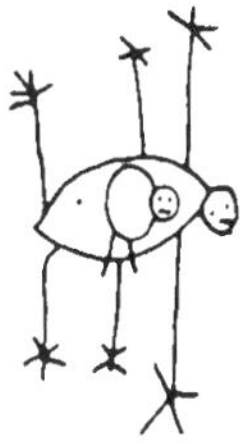

Fig. 112. Bavarian girl, 7 years (after Kerschensteiner). Horse and rider. Animal with a man's head (§31). Multiple legs which are folded out (§32). Rider drawn inside the horse (§68). Intellectual realism (§72).

Fig. 113. Simonne Luquet, French, 6;6 (Luquet collection). Cradle. Rabattement (§76).

ground, with those parts closest to the ground being the nearest to one another, and the higher ones the furthest away. Among a host of such examples, I will give that of a woman sitting in an armchair facing a cradle (fig. 114).

Fig. 114. Simonne Luquet, French, 5;6 (Luquet collection). Woman sitting in front of a cradle. Rabattement (§76).

Fig. 115. Jean Luquet, French, 7;6 (Luquet collection). Table and chair. Rabattement (§76).

In a drawing of a concert (fig. 68), the men in the orchestra and on the stage are folded out in an opposite direction from the audience to show that they are facing them. Similarly, the musician and his music stand, although really facing one another, are folded down opposite one another along an imaginary line drawn between them on the ground. For many different children, trees bordering the two sides of a road or path are spread out opposite one another along the axis of the route (fig. 116). The same happens in drawings of trees by a lake (fig. 76) or by a river (fig. 77); furthermore, in the former drawing, the boat and the two ducks are inverted with respect to the children who are facing them. In the courtyard of a house (fig. 117), the boy kicking the ball is turned upside-down to show that he has his back to the girl. A boy (6;4) drew a woman looking at herself in a three-panelled mirror (fig. 108), where the mirror and the woman are both shown from the front, but the mirror is drawn upside-down (as indicated by the suspension chain which the boy explicitly named). The same boy at seven-and-a-half, depicted the legs of a table and of a chair which were facing one another as pointing in opposite directions (fig. 115).

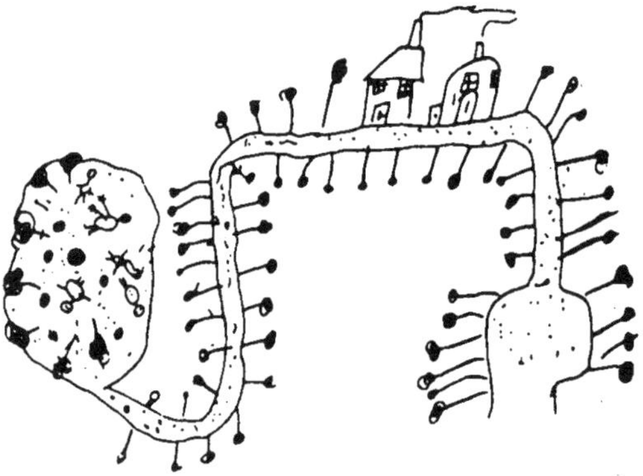

Fig. 116. Bavarian girl, 9 years (after Kerschensteiner). Children playing snowballs. Rabattement (§76).

The objects shown in rabattement can be set out not just in two parallel, vertical planes but in many more planes enclosing a polygon. Thus, in a drawing of a station (fig. 118), the main building and the two buildings at its side are folded out onto the ground, so that their vertical axes form a right angle as their facades do in reality; and the street light which stands in front of the central building and the central building itself are drawn upright, but the tram, which is parallel to the side buildings is turned on its side just as they are.

Finally, the area around which rabattement occurs can even be a circle, either real or virtual. Thus in the drawing of a circus (fig. 120), the benches and the musicians' platform (only one musician is shown), as well as the wires supporting the electric lamps and the poles to which they are attached are folded out in a circle around the circus ring. Often, the chairs around a table are shown in a similar way (fig. 52). In a drawing of a game of ring-a-roses,[19] the girls are spread out around the imaginary circle defined by their feet (fig. 121). In a roundabout drawn by a five-year-old Belgian boy, the people shown inside rectangular booths are lying down with their feet on the circular edge of the roundabout with their heads converging towards its centre (fig. 122).

Fig. 117. Simonne Luquet, French, 7;6 (Luquet collection). House with courtyard and garden. Rabattement for representing the children playing in the courtyard (§76). Mixture of viewpoints (§77).

77. These different techniques demonstrate the ingenuity of children and the power of intellectual realism. But what is even more remarkable is that children do not restrict themselves to one or other of these techniques but use them together in the same drawing. I will call this 'change of viewpoint' which is just an extension of exemplarity (§47). Having drawn an object from a viewpoint which presents its most characteristic aspect and which sets out the greatest number of its essential elements, the child then chooses to draw each of the rest of the details from a viewpoint which presents their exemplary forms. The combination of rabattement and plan view is

19. *'une ronde'*

an example of this; indeed, rabattement is in a sense only a change of viewpoint, since by moving around the object to be represented one can represent in elevation the vertical parts of the object in relation to the whole.

Fig. 118. Simonne Luquet, French, 6;6 (Luquet collection). Station. Rabattement (§76).

Fig. 119. The station drawn in fig. 118, based on a photograph.

Furthermore, the plan and elevation of the front or profile occur together in a host of drawings. In a number of drawings of houses, although the rooms are shown in plan view, the facade is represented in elevation with its door and windows, or is implied at least by the roof or the chimney. In drawings of houses with several floors, those shown in plan view are connected by a staircase in elevation, as in the drawing by a Californian girl (5;3) (fig. 124). The courtyards and gardens next to houses in elevation are shown in plan view, but with the flowers or shrubs and the doors in elevation

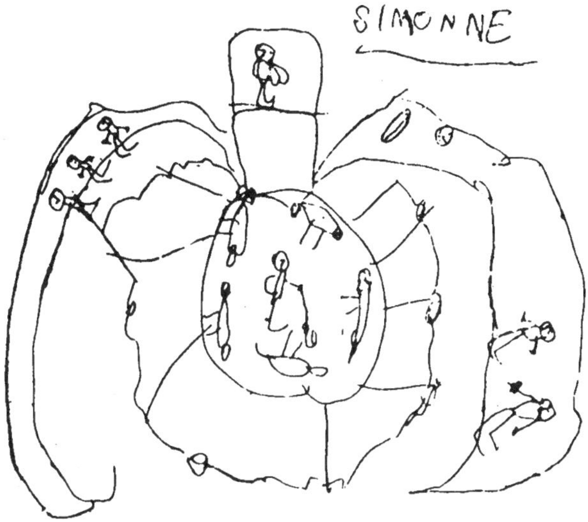

Fig. 120. Simonne Luquet, French, 5;6 (Luquet collection). Circus. Rabattement (§76).

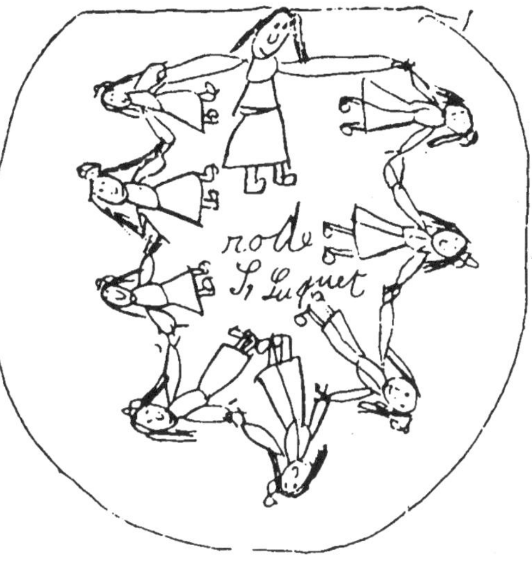

Fig. 121. Simonne Luquet, French, 7;6 (Luquet collection). Ring-a-roses [ronde]. Rabattement (§76).

(figs 73, 97, 117). Various children around the age of five when representing a door frontally, show the door knob not in frontal view within the rectangle of the door, but in profile on one of its vertical sides. In many drawings of prams (fig. 104) or beds (fig. 123) in profile, the people inside them are represented as though they were seen from above.

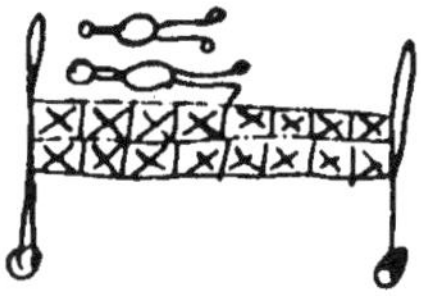

Fig. 122. Gabrielle, Belgian, 5 years (after Rouma). Roundabout. Rabattement (§76).

Fig. 123. Oliva, Belgian, 6 years (after Rouma). Bed. Mixture of viewpoints (§77).

Fig. 124. Ruth W., Californian, 5;3 (after Brown). House with three floors. Chairs, tables with pots of flowers, doors, staircase, windows, and bed. Changing viewpoint (§77).

In a drawing of an ancient gateway to a town, the two towers are shown in elevation, but almost everything else, and most notably the moat, is in plan. The benches along the central path are folded out on either side (fig. 125). For this drawing, as for figure 118, photographs of the corresponding objects are also presented to show how these two equally realistic representations – intellectual and visual realism – differ. In the chair at the top left of figure 68, the back of the seat and the front legs are seen frontally, the seat is seen from above, and the back legs which are inserted in the correct place at the join of the back and the seat are splayed out to each side, like the arms of an armchair. In a drawing of a boat (fig. 127), the hull

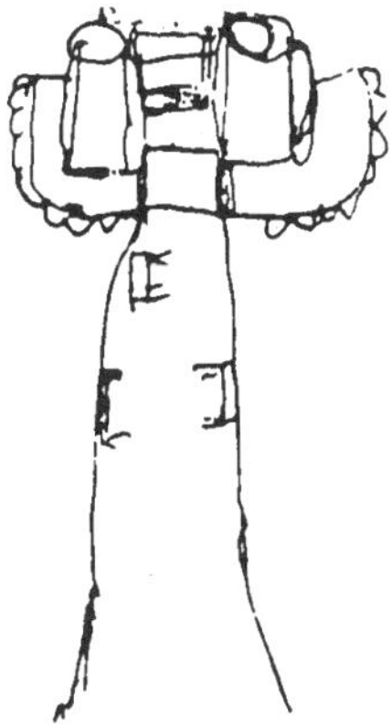

Fig. 125. Simonne Luquet, French, 6;6 (Luquet collection). Ancient town gate. Mixture of viewpoints (§77).

Fig. 126. The town gate drawn in fig. 125, based on a photograph.

of the boat is seen from above, the people from a viewpoint situated on the extension of the longitudinal axis of the boat, and the sails and rudder from a point along an extension of its transverse axis. A frequent type of horse-and-carriage drawing includes the shafts and the carriage in plan view, the wheels folded out on each side and the hood folded backwards (fig. 111). In many of their drawings of flowers in pots, children do not omit the small hole in the bottom for draining the water, even though it can only be seen from below (fig. 107). In drawings by children of many different nationalities of *Père Janvier* or *Saint Nicholas*, even though he is represented in frontal view, his sack of presents is on the side as if in profile, so that it is not hidden by his body (fig. 3).

Change of viewpoint also occurs in representations of living creatures. The noses of animals or people in profile are often shown with two nostrils, as if they were viewed from below. In many drawing of young girls, although they are shown facing forwards, the long hair or plaits that characterise these figures are shown in profile to make them show up clearly (fig. 109). It often happens that men shown in frontal view have their feet in profile, pointing in the same direction, presumably to avoid giving the impression that they are heading off in different directions (figs 101 and 131). Similarly, one finds a trunk in profile with a full-face head, a frontal trunk with everything else in profile (figs 101 and 128), arms in profile with the head full-face (fig. 129) or conversely the arms shown frontally with the head in profile (fig. 131). In a great many drawings, a nose in profile is added to a frontal view of the face (fig. 130), or else a face which is in profile nevertheless contains inside it either the mouth, the two eyes (fig. 99) or all of them together (figs 132 and 133); sometimes even an additional nose is added. A Belgian boy, when drawing a horse-rider, put two eyes inside the profile head of the rider yet just one on the head of the horse. When this discrepancy was pointed out to him, he abruptly added another eye to the horse. When trying to show the two eyes of a profile head, yet sensing the impossibility of putting both inside its outline, children will very occasionally resolve the problem by drawing one eye inside the head and the other outside. In a drawing of a horse in profile by a young boy (5;3) (fig. 134), one of the ears was drawn in the correct place but the other was drawn under the mouth, as if the ears had been viewed from above with one on each side. In the drawing of a horse and rider (fig. 89), by a seven-year-old Bavarian girl, the person was shown frontally and the horse mostly in profile, but the eyes were shown as if seen from above and the ears as if they were seen from the front.

Fig. 127. Simonne Luquet, French, 8;8 (Luquet collection). Boat. Changing viewpoint (§77).

As we have seen (§44), the same outline can sometimes represent a container and also its contents, such as an entire room and one of the items of furniture; it can also happen that the same contour may correspond to various aspects of an object seen from different viewpoints. Thus, in a drawing of a bedroom (fig. 135), the contour

Fig. 128. Belgian child, 6 years (after Rouma). Man, with front view of body, but with everything else in profile (§77).

Fig. 129. English boy, 5 years (after J. Sully). Man, with front view of face and arms in profile (§77).

Fig. 130. English boy, from 5 to 6 (after J. Sully). Man. Absence of arms (§46); hat in the air (§68); nose in profile but attached to a frontal view of the head (§77).

represents the floor since it contains the furniture, the walls since a wall cupboard and the chimney are attached to it, and the ceiling since the curtains of the window are attached to it at their top, indicated by curtain rods.

Fig. 131. English boy, 6 years (after J. Sully). Man. Top of the head visible under the hat; tacit correction rather than transparency (§74). Head and feet in profile, but with the body and arms shown frontally (§77).

Fig. 132. English boy, 5 to 6 years (after J. Sully). Man. Arms more primitive than the legs (§46). Eyes and mouth shown frontally, but the face in profile (§77).

78. So far, I have been summarising some of the diverse manifestations of children's perspective. It can be explained by a combination of a realist intention, which dominates all of children's drawings, and the synthetic sense, which characterises the stage we are now examining, unlike the previous stage involving synthetic incapacity. It is definitely realism, since the aim of all the techniques we have been considering is to provide the most faithful and complete representation of the object. But it is also if one looks more closely, a manifestation of the synthetic sense. At first sight, methods such as transparency, rabattement or change in viewpoint might seem to an adult to indicate a lack of any synthetic sense. An adult might insist that it is impossible to see all the features of an object at the same time, or the particular aspects they present. But this is to beg a more basic question as far as the child is concerned. It is to deny to drawing the possibility of any alternative to a visually-based synthesis which, after all, is really an abstraction, since it removes from the represented object everything that cannot be seen. Thus, instead of imposing *a priori* our laws upon child draughtsmen, we should try to understand the reason for the laws they impose upon themselves. And when we do this, we find that these laws conform

to a synthetic attitude, since they aim to combine in a single drawing the elements which are also combined in the object represented. Furthermore, rabattement serves to reveal the reciprocal relations between the folded-out elements.

Fig. 133. German boy, 7 years (after Levinstein). Man. No arms (§46). Face in profile, with details shown frontally, including a second nose.

Fig. 134. Jean Luquet, French, 5;3 (Luquet collection). Horse. Intellectual realism (§72). Changing viewpoint (§77).

79. It is the same concern for synthesis that eventually leads children, having invented for themselves intellectual realism as their mode of graphic representation, to abandon it just as spontaneously for the visual realism characteristic of adults' drawings.

Indeed, since the very essence of intellectual realism is to depict all the constituent elements of the object represented, it is able to portray all of them in relation to the overall object, regarded in its entirety as their common support. But having assembled all the elements, the drawing, in order to be completely realistic, also needs to convey the relations between each element and all the rest. However, these relations change with viewpoint, and so they cannot be shown in a coherent fashion unless the object is depicted from a single viewpoint, as perceived by the eye. For example, when two eyes are drawn in a picture of a head in profile, they cannot be placed either side of the nose. In order to render the objective state of affairs, it is necessary either to place one of the eyes outside the head, or else insert another nose between the eyes, thus giving the head two noses.

Intellectual realism thus gives rise to flagrant 'empirical' contradictions between the drawing and our experience. Children remain oblivious to these problems as long as their attention is completely taken up in the production of the drawing, not only while they are drawing but when they have finished. But with the development of their attentive capacity they come to apply their pre-existing critical faculty to their own work. Their repeated experiences then confirm the inevitable deficiencies of intellectual realism, and they reject it as a mode of graphic representation. In fact, the comments of many different children show that when they come to opt for visual realism this is a deliberate choice, and regarded henceforth as the one true form of realism. For example, a great many children when they show only one eye in their profile drawings explain that this is because the other one cannot be seen, and sometimes then turn over the paper to show where it would actually be.

If we take the representation of a single eye in profiles of heads as our criterion, the shift from intellectual to visual realism most often occurs between 8 and 9 years. But there are certainly great individual differences between children, and there is some evidence of an intention towards visual realism at much younger ages. For example, a young American girl (4;3) drew a cat with just one ear and then explained 'Just one ear; the other cannot be seen.' A young Californian boy (4;7) showed his drawing of a bee, and when he was asked where the legs were, he in turn asked 'Can you see the legs of bees when they are flying?' A German boy (4;8) drew a man in profile but slightly from behind so that one could see the back of the head and one eye at the side. When his parents, misunderstanding his intention, said 'The poor man! He has no mouth or nose', the boy placed himself in the position by almost turning his back towards them and asked 'When the man is like this, would you see his mouth? But you can see his eye.'

Visual realism excludes the various methods demanded by intellectual realism that we have already reviewed. When examining the chronological succession of these methods in the drawings by a single child, one finds that they disappear gradually, being sometimes used in drawings of a particular motif and sometimes falling out of use. Thus transparency gives way to occlusion, and the suppression of details which are in fact invisible. In the same way, rabattement and change in viewpoint are replaced by perspective and their equivalents in visual realism. Buildings, for example, begin to be shown in three-quarter view. Perspective changes the appearance of outlines or details of objects viewed frontally, so that a circular shape viewed from the side projects an ellipse extended vertically, and one viewed from above projects an ellipse extended horizontally. As a result, visual realism leads to the abandonment of exemplarity of form. One even finds, if very rarely, examples of the most outrageous foreshortening if it is required by the motif. Thus, a drawing by a girl of five-and-a-half represented a child lying on his back, with his legs in the air, as an illustration of the song 'Have you seen the moon, my lad? If you haven't, here it is!' (fig. 136).[20]

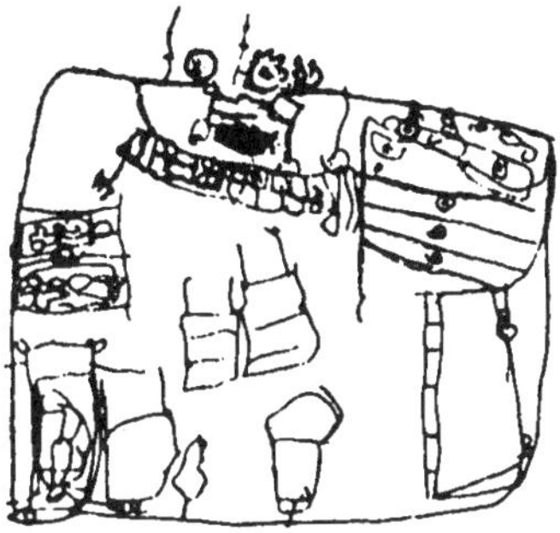

Fig. 135. Simonne Luquet, French, 5;6 (Luquet collection). Bedroom. Changing viewpoint: a single contour for different surfaces of the same object (§77).

Fig. 136. Simonne Luquet, French, 7;6 (Luquet collection). Child viewed from underneath with legs in the air. Foreshortening (§79).

But the replacement of intellectual realism by visual realism, any more than the acquisition of the synthetic sense (§70), does not occur in a single stroke. Visual realism has to struggle against some firmly entrenched habits, and it is not firmly established once it has appeared. Intellectual realism not only reappears in later drawings, but the same drawing may include aspects of visual realism and intellectual realism. For example, in drawings of houses by children of many different nationalities, the furniture continues to be shown in transparency even when the inhabitants are only partly visible through the windows. In drawings of flowers in pots, even though the roots are no longer depicted in transparency, the drainage hole in the bottom of the pot continues to be represented, even though it is not visible from the side. Animals in profile still have two nostrils, in accord with intellectual realism, while, at the same time, they are given just one eye, in accord with visual realism (fig. 92). Furthermore, in drawings which include several people or animals in

20. The French title of the song is: 'As-tu vu la lune, mon gars? Si tu n'l'as pas vue, la voilà!' The song is presumably about 'mooning'.

profile, some have just one eye, sometimes accompanied by the explanation that the other one is on the other side of the head, and so cannot be seen, yet the others are shown with two eyes.

One curious drawing (fig. 137) demonstrates an intention towards visual realism: a bird perched in a tree and being stalked by the eagle is not shown, since, as the child explicitly states, 'it is hidden in one of the trees and you cannot see it'. Yet several other characteristics of this drawing still conform to intellectual realism. The hunter is shown frontally but the arm holding the bow aimed at the eagle is in profile (exemplarity of form and change in viewpoint). The point of the arrow, which as the streams of blood explicitly indicate has gone into the eagle, is represented in transparency.

Fig. 137. Jean Luquet, French, 6;4 (Luquet collection). Man shooting an arrow at an eagle. The persistence of intellectual realism in visual realism (§79). Graphic narration: successive type with repetition of elements (§83).

Furthermore, even in drawings where intellectual realism does not occur, it often happens that visual realism although attempted is not achieved, and the perspective is faulty. The main reason is that children generally draw without a model rather than from nature, if only because otherwise they would often have to abandon the drawing to go and look at the object they are drawing. In addition, they do not know the laws of perspective. Since the perspective they apply to their drawings is based neither on immediate observation nor on scientific construction, they can only rely upon often distant visual memories of the represented object or else objects which are roughly similar. For example, in several drawings by Munich school children, a tram was shown with its roof as if it had been seen not from ground-level but from above, even though they had never had the opportunity to look at trams from this viewpoint. They therefore imagined the perspective, most probably on the basis of everyday objects which can be seen from above, such as packing cases standing on the ground, low cupboards, boxes placed on a table, or toy trams or railway carriages. It is easy to see why the use of such different visual memories in constructing the perspective of a particular object does not at first lead to a coherent synthesis.

This is very clear in drawings of houses. Children clearly must have noticed that the far side of the house is invisible, and only in exceptional cases do they include it in their drawings. But they have seen houses in three-quarter view where either the left or right side is seen together with the front, and it takes them time to realise that they have never seen the two sides of the house at the same time. Consequently, they often draw houses with three sides (fig. 138).

The representation of a roof can also gives rise to problems. Children encounter several different kinds of roofs. Thus some have four pitched sides, each extending above one of the rectangular sides of the house. Now, all four sides of a roof can be triangular, converging towards a single point, or else there can be two trapezoidal sides which join to form a ridge to the ends of which are connected two triangular sides. Furthermore, there are roofs with just two pitched sides that are connected to two opposite sides of the house, whereas the two remaining sides of the house extend beyond the others to the top of the roof. Such roofs can either have the gables at the front and back or at the sides. So it is not surprising that children confuse these different types of roof, each of which actually exists. Often, children are content to add triangles to the two sides of a house (fig. 138), without realising that the different sides of the roof have to connect at the top to form a continuous covering.

Errors of perspective of this kind (not to mention aerial perspective) can only be corrected through practice in drawing from nature. Among peoples lacking a specialised graphic culture, such errors continue well beyond childhood. For example, a twenty-year-old Bolivian, who was both intelligent and cultivated, drew a house with three sides very similar to that drawn by a child of seven-and-a-half (fig. 138). This is by no means unusual, and when one submits the drawings of adults to the same close analysis as children's drawings, one can quickly gather a host of drawings that hardly differ from those of children of around twelve years old, and can be even worse. Some drawings by adults have not even passed the stage of intellectual realism, such as birds whose heads are distinct from their bodies, contrary to their visual appearance, or even man drawings where two eyes are drawn inside a profile head.

Fig. 138. Jean Luquet, French, 7;4 (Luquet collection). House struck by lightning. Intention determined by external circumstances (§8).

Eventually, even if for some individuals it may be later rather than sooner, the period of children's drawings comes to an end. Its end is marked by the renunciation of intellectual realism as a mode of graphic representation, through the firm resolve to conform to visual appearances, even though various obstacles prevent this intention from being fully attained.

10
Graphic Narration

80. So far I have been considering drawings which correspond to static scenes. Such drawings show an object either by itself or in relation to several other objects, and, objectively, the view they represent could be taken in at a single glance. But our visual experience is not only of static or instantaneous scenes but also of dynamic or changing events, involving a succession of moments, where each resembles what went before in some respects while differing in others. I will call a drawing of this kind 'graphic narration' since it depicts an event by traces just as a story would describe it in words.

Once the drawing is finished, all of the elements depicted are simultaneously visible, and those not included are, of course, completely absent. The reality that the drawing represents, however, is a combination of permanent elements of the event that could be continually seen and changing elements that succeed one another, and some of these changing elements could only appear once the others had already ceased to appear. The problem posed by graphic narration is therefore as follows. How can a drawing, where all the elements are simultaneously present and unchanging, represent an event where some elements were replaced by others while others remained fixed? In other words, how is it possible to represent an event occurring over time so that the successive moments maintain a relation of continuity between one another?

81. There are three solutions to this problem. The first two are employed by both children and adults, but the third is special to children. The first involves selecting just one phase of the action or episode of the story as the most important and using this to symbolise the entire event. So I will call this first mode of graphic narration the *symbolic type*. This type, which is widely used by professional illustrators, is also used by children. An especially clear example comes from a boy just under seven years old, who lived on a ranch in Southern California and had received no training in

drawing; he had written a small book of stories, including the following one: 'One day, Ralph went out to go to the barn. He heard a great noise. He ran to see what was going on. All the cattle were running in all directions. He saw a big bear. He ran home and warned his father. His father came and killed the bear.' This narrative was illustrated by a drawing representing just one of the scenes from the story, that of the cattle running in all directions, with the bear in the background (fig. 139).

Fig. 139. Californian boy, under 7 years (after Barnes). Cattle fleeing from a bear. Graphic narration of the symbolic type (§81).

82. A second mode of graphic narration differs from the symbolic type in that it does not represent the story by a single image symbolising the entire event. Instead, there are several complete images each depicting one of the moments, and each sufficing in itself to represent the corresponding episode, just as the single image

Fig. 140. English girl, 8 years (after Levinstein). Alice and Peter the Gander. Graphic narration: Epinal type (§82).

of the symbolic type represents the entire event. This is the technique used in Epinal images, and so I will call it the *Epinal type*.[21]

Some children's drawings are just like Epinal images: they are divided into separate squares or rectangles, and sometimes they are accompanied by some text or by numbers indicating the sequence of the images. In other drawings, the images are less clearly distinguished from one another. Sometimes there is just a horizontal or vertical line separating adjacent images, and sometimes these dividing lines are not even present and the images are simply juxtaposed. But in every case, an Epinal type of drawing is characterised by the combination of several constituent images each corresponding to a different moment in the story. Among examples from children of different nationalities, I have chosen a drawing by an eight-year-old English girl, representing the story entitled 'Alice and Peter the Gander' (fig. 140). It includes eight numbered pictures, where the first two are separated by a vertical line and the rest are simply juxtaposed. In the first three, the line of the ground also serves as the line of demarcation. The episodes of the story, represented by their characteristic elements, are as follows: (1) Alice with her pet gander; (2) Alice playing with a hoop and going away from the house without checking that Peter was not following her as she had been told to do; (3) Edward with his dog Nero; (4) Edward stopping by a hedge beside a fence to cut off a stick, while Nero notices Peter (this episode is represented merely by the fence); (5) Nero leaping on Peter, who, being seized by the wing, struggles and shreaks; (6) Edward arriving with his stick to make Nero let go; (7) Alice taking Peter in her arms and returning home; (8) Alice and Peter having gone back into the house.

83. Since there is no other possibility than that the drawing be composed either of just one image or several, it would seem *a priori* that the symbolic and Epinal types ought to exhaust all the options, and this is the case for the aesthetics of us adults. But this is not the case for children, and a number of their drawings are of a different and very distinctive and readily identifiable type. Unlike the Epinal type, but just like the symbolic type, it includes a single image. But whereas each of the constituent images of the Epinal type only contains elements that could be seen at any one time, this third type of graphic narration combines elements which objectively belong to

21. Epinal images are named after a centre of production of popular illustrations, characterised by their bright colours and use of strip cartoons.

different moments of the event or, to be more precise, elements which could only be seen in succession. I therefore call it the *successive type*.

There are two varieties. In the first, the unchanging elements of the event are drawn just once, whereas the changing elements (the main actors, incidental characters who intervene at a given moment but then disappear, and perhaps the 'scenery') are shown several times, each of their representations corresponding to one of their different locations. For this reason, I call this the successive type *with* repetition.

Here are some examples from children of different nationalities. A class of Belgian school children was asked to represent a story they had been told about a person stealing birds' eggs who had been killed when he fell from a tree. Four of the children produced a similar drawing: the tree is shown just once; the person is represented five times in successive positions: at two points up the trunk of the tree, on a branch near to the nest, falling head first, and then laid out on the ground after the fall. In a drawing of a shop by a French girl (5;6), a woman (A1) talks to the shop-keeper (B1) and tells him she has seen the doll in the bed. The shop-keeper goes to get it (B2), then to the cash desk with the woman's money (B3), then comes back to her (B4), bringing back the doll to her in one hand and the change in the other. In A2, the woman is in the street, carrying her parcel (fig. 141). As one can see, the 'scene' is shown just once, but the people appear each time they perform a different action. Similarly, in a drawing about the story of Blue-Beard by an Irish boy of eight in a school in California (fig. 142), the actors are shown several times or just once depending on whether they change at all. Sister Ann is shown once for the two episodes of the herd of sheep and the approach of the brothers, because during these two episodes she remains on the ridge of the roof observing what is going on. Blue-Beard is shown three times in three different situations: once with his wife, when he forbids her from looking into the closet; once when he is preparing to cut off her head for disobeying; and finally in his coffin in the hearse. Mrs Blue-Beard is shown twice, corresponding to the two scenes I have just mentioned where she is with her husband, and a third time corresponding to the intermediate scene where she goes into the closet.

In a drawing by a ten-year-old German boy, representing the story of John Nose-in-the-Air, the hero is shown no less than six times: 1. Going towards the dog; 2. falling over the dog; 3. walking beside

Fig. 141. Simonne Luquet, French, 5;6 (Luquet collection). Woman in a shop. Graphic narration: successive type with repetition of elements (§83).

the water; 4. falling into the water; 5. having fallen in; 6. heading for the life buoy that has been thrown to him.

The changing elements in a story may not be just the main and incidental characters, but also objects, and these too may be repeated in the drawing. For example, a Belgian boy (4;6) was drawing while making up his own story. A 'nasty man' with a knife in his hand is chasing a young girl who is pushing a barrow; a policeman intervenes with his sword and arrests the culprit; in their struggle they upset the barrow. The barrow is shown twice, once in its normal position, being pushed by the girl, and then turned over, with its wheels in the air.

In a drawing by a French boy (6;4), representing a man shooting an arrow at an eagle, the arrow is shown twice, first in the bow and then having hit the eagle (fig. 137). Another French boy (5;6) drew a waterchute. The boat is first shown at the top, then in two successive positions along the inclined surface along which it is sliding, then falling into the water which splashes all around it, and finally hanging from the cable which will draw it up again to recommence its descent (fig. 143). In a drawing by a ten-year-old girl from Munich of children throwing snowballs, different snowballs

Fig. 142. Irish boy (8 years) in a school in California (after Barnes). Blue-Beard. Absence of clothes (§46). Representation of the navel (§52). Double transparency (§74). Repetition variant of the successive type of graphic narration (§83).

are shown several times in their successive positions, linked by a line corresponding to their trajectory. More often, the moving object is shown once, but its trajectory is indicated by a line. This is the case in drawings by children from Breslau representing the country of Cocagne which show the trajectories of the roasted larks falling into the mouths of the inhabitants of that charmed country. A four-year-old Californian girl explained while she was drawing the details of a watch: 'This is a watch; this is the hand, which turns like this', and she depicted the movement of the hand by a roughly circular trace extending from its middle (fig. 53).

84. In the second variant of the successive type, those elements which in the actual event occur in succession are again combined

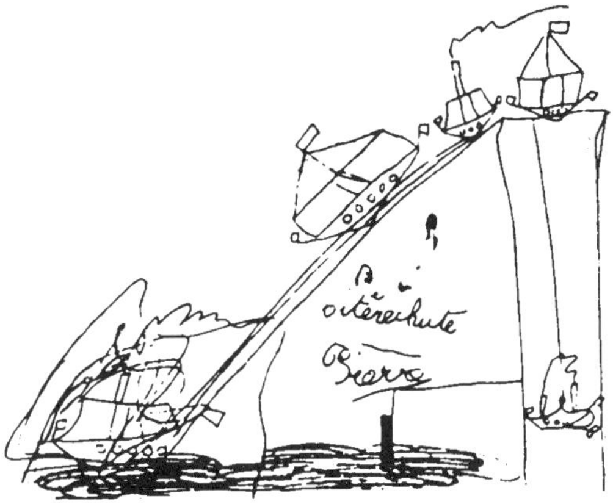

Fig. 143. Pierre R., French, 5;6 (Luquet collection). Waterchute. Graphic narration: successive type with repetition of elements (§83).

Fig. 144. American boy, 9 years (after Barnes). John Nose-in-the-Air. Graphic narration: successive type without repetition of elements (§83).

in a single image, but in this case no element is depicted more than once; hence, it is appropriate to call this the successive type *without* repetition. For example, a nine-year-old American boy, representing the story of John Nose-in-the-Air, juxtaposed John viewed from the back, the sun, the moon surrounded by stars, a dog, a river and three fish (fig. 144). A drawing by another American boy, who was eight years old, showing the story of Jack and the Beanstalk, combined three successive moments: Jack cutting the beanstalk with an axe, the giant falling to the ground, and the wife of the giant crying about the death of her husband (fig. 145). A drawing by a five-year-old

Belgian boy represented the following subject: a man smashing the electric bulb of a street lamp by throwing stones. The police arrest him, and take him to the police station where 'his name is taken down' and finally he is put into prison. In this drawing, the main character is shown just once, at the moment when he is throwing the stones at the lamp. He is not shown in any of the later scenes: in the police station only the policemen are shown, and in the prison only the 'thieves' with whom he is incarcerated are shown (fig. 146).

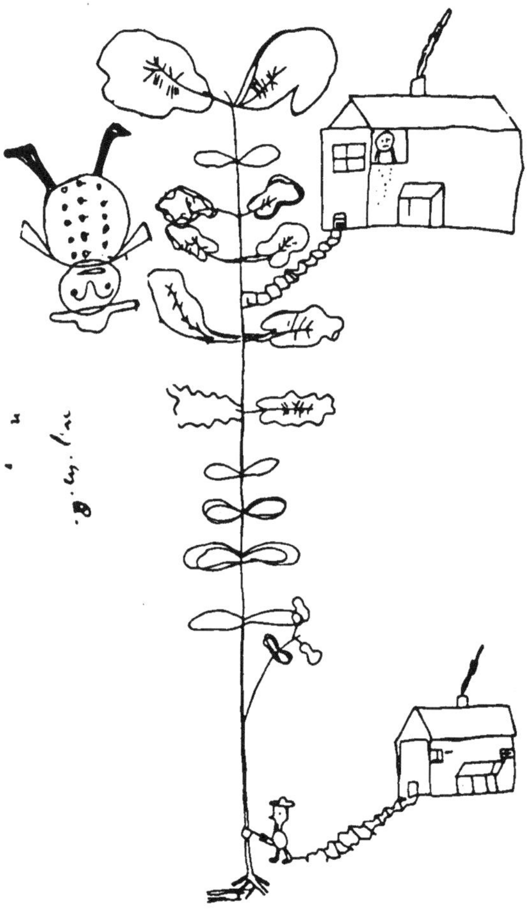

Fig. 145. American boy, 8 years (after Barnes). Jack and the Beanstalk. Graphic narration: successive type without repetition (§83).

Fig. 146. Gustave, Belgian, 5 years (after Rouma).
Story of the smashing of an electric lamp. Graphic narration:
successive type without repetition (§84).

85. As one can see, the distinctive characteristics of the different types of graphic narration used by children are very distinct and can be easily recognised by simple inspection of any drawing. Whereas the Epinal type contains several distinct images, the others comprise just one. In the symbolic type, all the details shown in the drawing relate to the same moment in the story and they thus would have all been visible at the same time. The successive type combines within a single image details (people or objects) which in reality could only have been perceived at separate times: in the variant without repetition, all the elements are different, whereas in the variant with repetition, some of the elements are depicted more than once.

On the basis of their distinctive characteristics, these different types can be ordered according to how much they conform to visual experience and its logic, and, conversely, to the extent to which they capture the inherent continuity of the whole temporal event. The symbolic type presents to the observer a scene that conforms to what would have been visible at a given instant, but it substitutes for the continuous succession of the event just one single image. In other words, it eliminates from the depicted story precisely that which makes it a story rather than a mere static episode.

The Epinal type presents several images, and hence is richer than the symbolic type. It also conforms to a large extent to visual experience since each of the images, like the single image of the symbolic type, only contains details which in reality could be seen at the same time. Although the drawing as a whole combines in a single glance details which did not in fact occur at the same time, their succession is indicated by various devices (frames or lines of separation, and numbers). On the other hand, it neglects the continuity of identity of elements in the represented story, since whatever remains the same over time, be it a person or the setting, is shown several times across the separate images, even though to the mind it is a single entity.

The successive type is better at evoking the continuity of the action since it combines in a single image details which in fact belong to different times. On the other hand, it conflicts with visual experience since these successive instants could never be seen at the same time. The variant without repetition, however, fails to differentiate between those details which change from moment to moment and those which persist, since either kind is shown just the once. It is the variant with repetition that captures in the fullest possible way the two antagonistic factors involved in continuity: identity and change. The details which change are distinguished by being repeated whilst the stable elements are shown only the once. This is the type, therefore, that most closely approaches continuity, but at the same time it is the most distant from visual experience, since it simultaneously portrays not only successive elements (as indeed does the variant without repetition), but also one and the same detail in different situations.

In short, we encounter in the representation of dynamic events,[22] as we did earlier for representations of static scenes, the same opposition between visual and intellectual realism. The first aims to represent the subject as the eye of the artist has seen it, and the second as how the artist's mind knows it to be. The *mind* is aware of continuity over time, since while looking at an event, it is aware that each view gives rise to others, which, though different in certain respects, also resemble one another since they relate to the same event.[23] In contrast, the *eye* does not sense the continuity, since, like a movie camera, each instantaneous 'frame' has neither a before nor after, but is entirely limited to the instant when it is seen. Thus for the graphic representation of duration of dynamic events, intellectual realism shows change as we experience it in our minds,

22. 'la représentation des tableauz dynamiques'
23. '*drame*'

as an inextricable combination of identity and difference. In contrast, visual realism, like a cinematic film, fragments the continuity into a succession of discontinuous instants by eliminating from each instant its relation to earlier and later instants. Visual realism rules out the very possibility that a single drawing, seen in a single glance, could combine several successive instants or several representations of the same object.

The idea of duration or temporal continuity involves a fundamental fusion of identity and difference, or persistence and change. The successive type *with* repetition thus corresponds to the purest intellectual realism, since it portrays an event by combining within the same drawing stable elements which are represented a single time and changing elements which are represented every time they change. In doing so, however, it runs counter to visual experience, since the same object cannot appear more than once at the same time. The variant *without* repetition avoids this problem by representing any object or person just once, but while it approaches visual realism in this respect, it still presents to a single glance elements that do not in fact occur at the same time. This contradiction is eliminated by the Epinal type, since the successive instants are separated from one another within the overall drawing and each corresponds to a distinct image which is sufficient in itself. The constituent images, although they are separated, are still juxtaposed, however, within a single drawing. Finally, the symbolic type corresponds to the purest visual realism, since it includes no more than one image, and all the details would be simultaneously visible in reality.

86. Having listed the different types of graphic narration found among children's drawings, there remains the question of whether children resort to any of these types just as they wish, or whether they move from one to another in a definite order according to their age.

The available data are still too limited and fragmentary to allow any complete answer. For example, it is not possible to determine if the two variants of the successive type are used at the same time, or in succession. However, the facts seem to indicate that the symbolic type is not used to any significant extent until about 11 or 12 years, after the period of children's drawings in the strict sense. During this period, graphic narration is almost exclusively based on the successive and the Epinal types, and there is a definite and progressive replacement of the first type by the second around 8 years. Until that age, many children can make no sense of Epinal images, even very simple ones composed of just two images. Even when they are told that the images represent the same story, or, even more explicitly, that the same characters are shown in the different images, they still take them to be different people.

The substitution of the successive type by the Epinal type corresponds to a fragmentation of temporal continuity into discontinuous instants, and hence the replacement of intellectual realism by visual realism. Thus in graphic narration, as in the representation of static scenes, children as they grow up abandon one conception of realism for another.

Conclusions: Psychological and Educational

Psychological Conclusions

87. Drawing passes successively through four phases or periods for all modern civilised people.[24] Children are well aware that drawings by other people represent objects, and they themselves are able to draw lines, but initially they do not know how to draw lines to represent objects. It is only later, when they discover that the lines they themselves have drawn can fortuitously resemble objects, that they begin to have the intention to draw in order to represent things. The purposive character of drawing in the strict sense only arises once fortuitous realism has been replaced by intentional realism.

After that major event, the subsequent phases of drawing only differ in the way they achieve this realist intention. In the second period, this realist intention is hindered by various difficulties which can conceal it from an observer, and the principle feature of this phase of failed realism is synthetic incapacity. During this period, children are unable to organise the various details into a coherent whole because while they are drawing they are completely preoccupied with depicting each detail in itself.

Once this difficulty has been surmounted, drawing reaches the third phase, which is the culmination of children's drawing. This stage is characterised by intellectual realism. In this stage, children are aiming, deliberately and, no doubt, consciously, at reproducing the represented object not just as it can be seen, but precisely as 'it is', and they give each detail its exemplary form.

Finally, in the fourth period, drawing attains visual realism of which the principle manifestation is the submission to perspective, even if it is poorly executed. From that point, children have, in their drawing, reached the adult period. Only development in technical skill,

24. Although Luquet talks of *four* stages: fortuitous realism, failed realism, intellectual realism, and visual realism, his account commences with an initial stage of 'pure trace-making' engaged in just for the sheer pleasure of making marks rather than creating a resemblance to something else.

acquired in a specialised culture, establishes differences among individuals, and many adults remain incapable throughout their lives of producing drawings any different from those of children of 10 or 12.

88. The theoretical distinction I have drawn between these four phases of drawing is in fact much less clear in practice. Each stage persists after the following one has already begun. This is true not only for children but also for adults who complacently believe they have reached the phase of visual realism, for sporadic traces of intellectual realism continue to appear in their drawings. There is an analogy here with what Auguste Comte noted in relation to his law of the three stages of human knowledge: individuals who have attained in some respects the 'positive' state of knowledge remain in other respects in the metaphysical or even theological state.

The individual development of drawing, like any other modification in our activity, is subject to regressions. According to Ribot's law of regression, when people lose previously acquired memories or habits, these disappear in a definite order, the opposite to that in which they were acquired. However, in the case of retraining, be it spontaneous or assisted, reacquisition occurs in the same order as the original acquisition. Children's drawings, in the development of different graphic types, conform to this law. When certain details previously included disappear in a later drawing of the same subject (because, for example, the child is concentrating instead on some new detail being depicted for the first time), the details omitted are those which have appeared most recently. If children have not drawn a certain subject for some time, they may even forget the graphic type. When this type reappears, the drawings of this subject are quite rudimentary and similar to its very first examples.

89. Children's drawings lend themselves to some very interesting comparisons. On the one hand, considered as testimony of a more or less explicit conception of the function of figurative drawing, they can be compared to prehistoric art, to the art of savage peoples, and to the earliest periods of ancient and modern art. These together form a much vaster genre of primitive art. I must limit myself here to this brief comment, but it provides the subject for a book in its own right.[25]

On the other hand, children's drawings reflect and therefore provide evidence of their psychology, and thereby allow us to determine in what ways they resemble the adult and how they differ.

25. Luquet discussed these wider relations more fully in several publications, including *L'art primitif* (1930).

In connection with the factors of intention and interpretation of drawings, we have been able to see the role of external circumstances, of association of ideas and analogy, and of imagination. In addition, drawings provide us to some extent with an index of the child's mental image of any object, or, as I have called it, the internal model since it is a representation of how the object appears to the child at the time he or she is drawing it. Realism, which is a constant feature of children's drawings, demonstrates the sharpness of their observation. After all, the very attempt to depict objects in such scrupulous detail requires that the child observe it very carefully. On the other hand, in many cases the drawing (and therefore the internal model) is not meant to represent an individual object or person, but a category of objects. It is a generic image, the visual equivalent to a general idea. In this way, children's drawings prove that children are capable of generalisation. Furthermore, the phenomenon I have called exemplarity shows that generalisation, for children and adults alike, involves taking an individual as typifying a class of similar entities, and thus reconciles both the nominalist and the conceptualist theories of generalisation. We can thus accept the formula of La Bruyère that children are already 'small adults': their mental mechanism shares, as it were, the same clockwork and source of energy.

90. Accordingly, I believe there is a need to challenge a quite unfair judgment generally held among those who have written about children's drawings. Among the mental characteristics of children, there is hardly anything more prominent than the commitment to routine. I have already noted this trait. This is manifest in the conservation of type, when it prevents the development of realism or hinders the analogical transfer of progress already achieved for one motif to a motif currently being drawn. It is also manifest in the persistence of certain features of an earlier phase of drawing, such as synthetic incapacity or intellectual realism, even though the subsequent stage of drawing development has already begun. But although the facts themselves are clear, they do not, in my view, justify the unfavourable explanation that has been given, that this commitment to routine derives exclusively from laziness. One might say that children spare themselves the effort of modifying their types and their methods. Admittedly, mental laziness in both children and adults is one of the causes of routine. But the simple fact of the modification of type and the spontaneous development of drawing demonstrate that in a host of cases, when

children discover some innovation, or have one suggested to them, they eagerly take it up, as long as their mental development allows them to benefit from it. Overall, then, when they conserve types and procedures, it is to satisfy their current state of mind, and their commitment to conservation is proof, not of their laziness, but their resolve. We should not forget that even the routine of children is far from passive. It involves a struggle against the examples and suggestions given by adults, even though it would probably be easier for children to give in to such influences than remain true to their own ways. Furthermore, the phenomenon of duplicity of types, where children produce different drawings of the same subject depending on whether the drawing is intended to satisfy themselves or for someone else, indicates that they are ceaselessly vigilant in trying to maintain their own originality. Finally, even if there could be some doubt about such originality in relation to the conservation of types, it is unquestionable in relation the creation of types. Children actively reconstruct the data provided by their perceptions, selecting those details to omit and those to include. When drawing they replace their raw perceptual impressions with an internal model of the object, and this is just as true for their drawings from nature and copied drawings, as for their drawings from memory.

91. This conclusion has great significance for general psychology. Children are already human beings, even if they are at the very outset of being human, and so childhood is where one can discover the origins of mind and what is innate. As a consequence, children's drawings provide incontestable evidence against the empiricist conception of mental life. According to that doctrine, mental representations should simply copy empirical realities conveyed by sensory impressions, supposedly imposed upon a compliant and purely receptive mind.

Associationism is a more specific form of empiricism, in that it adds mental atomism to the assumption of the passivity of mind. Mental representations deriving from external stimulation are supposed to be formed through addition or synthesis. For example, we experience one sensed quality, and then another, and it is only after they have been experienced as isolated sensations, that, through being experienced together, they form a perception. These individual perceptions in turn are supposed to form general ideas, and so forth.

The specific doctrine of assocationism is intimately linked with the general thesis of empiricism. Indeed, if one accepts the associationist assumption that more complex mental states are simply formed from less complex elements, the mind is merely a passive container and makes no more contribution to their production than does a test-tube to the chemical reactions occurring inside it. On this view, mental phenomena occur within the mind but without its intervention. Thus the mental atomism of associationism repeats the general empiricist thesis of the passivity of the mind.

These two linked conceptions of mental life are both challenged by the actual development of children's drawings. The internal model as it is translated onto paper by the graphic movements of the infant is nothing other than the corresponding visual representation of the object being drawn as it exists in the mind of the child. Now, according to the general conception of empiricism, the passivity of the mind should cause the internal model simply to be a copy of the represented object. Yet even drawings presenting individual rather than generic images, which should demand the highest fidelity in the copy, do not conserve all the visible elements or details of real objects. The analysis or abstraction by which only certain elements are conserved in the internal model is a selection guided by the importance children give to the elements, and the interest they take in them. Thus, at the very outset of childhood, the mind is far from purely receptive, but is, instead, active in a fundamental way in elaborating what is presented to it.

If we now consider the thesis of mental atomism, linked to associationism, then, according to this doctrine, children's drawings should progress chronologically from the parts to the whole and from the individual to the general. Yet this is exactly the reverse of what actually occurs. On the first point, it is easy to confirm that the development of the internal model goes, not from the parts to the whole, but from the whole to the parts. Admittedly, as I have already indicated, association plays a role in the appearance of certain details, and I have also stressed that children at first proceed by simple juxtaposition of details and thus seem, as a consequence of their inability to connect the details, to support the associationists. However, if at the beginning they have difficulty in capturing in their drawing – and no doubt in their internal model – the entire image of an object with its various elements, this hardly means that these elements were originally perceived as separate and only later integrated. Would one say of a child who drew a horse with legs at one corner of the paper and the head at the other that he first saw only the legs, and only after that the head? In fact, a variety of factors, including the association of ideas, attract the child's attention to one and then another element of the whole, yet each of these elements implies the undifferentiated whole. The element that attracts the child's attention is just a part of the whole that happens to be more clearly highlighted at that particular time. For example, children's earliest drawings of houses could hardly be said to involve a synthesis of images of separate rooms: the kitchen, the dining room, bedroom, etc. Indeed, in a series of drawings of this subject by one child, it was the entire house that first appeared, and only later did one room and then another become differentiated within the whole. Furthermore, when a second room appears in a drawing of a house beside an initial one, such as a dining room beside a kitchen, it is not really added to the kitchen as such, but to the house which is, as it were, primarily a kitchen. Starting with a confused representation of the whole, the child moves towards a distinct representation of this totality by concentrating on all of the constituent elements in succession. Underlying each of the elements, to the extent that they enter clearly into consciousness, there remains the representation of the whole from which it derives. If it were a case of the mere successive registration of isolated details, devoid of any sense that they are just parts of the whole, then it is difficult to see why the details that are first reproduced are the most significant, since their significance relative to the others already implies a comparison among all the details, and hence an awareness of the whole.

Furthermore, how could we explain the fact that certain details are regarded as the most essential, as constituting the 'substance' of the object in some way encapsulating or symbolising the totality? In short, the gradual increase of depicted details which constitutes the knowledge of the type seems to me to occur in most cases not by addition or juxtaposition, but through division, discrimination, or evolution in Herbert Spencer's sense of differentiation. In my opinion, association in the strict sense intervenes only in relatively rare cases, namely when the child shifts from a simple motif to a more complex one through the addition of a new detail to a previously self-contained drawing.

Drawings depicting individual subjects differentiated by distinctive details only appear after a certain time. For example, children draw a church before any particular church, a house before their own house, people before individual people. Even when their drawings are inspired by a particular object, the individual image is often only the symbol of a more general representation (I have already discussed this in terms of 'exemplarity'). When drawing a house where the details are those of her own, a girl does not say 'This is our house', but 'This is like our house.' If individual details only appear in children's drawings after the generic elements, we have to conclude that in the internal model of the earliest drawings these details have been eliminated, or more exactly put aside into a dark corner from which they will only come to emerge at a later time. As I have already discussed, among the different visible characteristics of the same object, children impose a hierarchy of value based on the importance they attribute to them. There is also another hierarchy based on the degree of their generality. The development of drawing demonstrates that individual details only attract the visual attention of children after the generic characteristics: not only do they see the general in the particular, but they even see the individual as general before they see it as individual. Again, these facts run counter to associationist theory. Children, and hence the human mind, progresses not only from the whole to its parts, but also from the general to the individual. Furthermore, in many cases, the passage from the whole to the parts and that from the general to the individual are one and the same: thus the details which distinguish a man drawing reduced to its essentials from a more elaborate drawing are those which distinguish one person from another: their clothing, their gestures, etc. One can apply to graphic images what logicians teach about ideas: the wider their extension the less their 'distinctiveness'.[26]

92. In my view, the study of children's drawings allows us to discern the profound analogy or essential kinship between the psychology of the child and that of the adult. There are also differences, however, that pertain to the special conditions of childhood. The first of these differences I will mention only briefly since it is of an extrinsic kind, and hence liable to vary considerably between individuals: children live in an artificial environment in that society and the family take care of them. The more important difference is intrinsic and essential, since it derives from the fact that children are at the very outset of their lives. They still have not

26. The term used in formal logic would be 'intension' or 'comprehension'. For example, although the content (extension) of the class of 'boats' is more inclusive than that of 'steam boats', the latter class has a more differentiated or distinctive definition.

benefited from the lessons of experience, unless in the form of inherited traces, and hence they have to do by instinct what adults achieve by reflection.

As a result, the study of childhood provides an entry into what could be called the metaphysics of psychology. In other publications, I have indicated the extent to which considerations about finality ought to enter into the explanation of psychological reality, and the way in which this metaphysical notion can take on a positive meaning, quite as consistent with a purely mechanistic conception of the universe as with the hypothesis of Providence or of a benevolent Nature. Everyone who is alive has had everything he or she needs to survive. In other words, both our biological and psychological organisation have been constantly adapted to their conditions of existence, and hence the notion of conditions of existence is the empirical and incontestable equivalent of that of finality.

These general considerations, which relate both to psychology in general and also to the psychology of thinking (or in other words, logic) apply equally to childhood, in terms of drawing. Childhood is not just the beginning of life, but also its apprenticeship, and so the mental mechanisms of children need to be adapted to the preservation of their lives throughout childhood and into adulthood.

First of all, the very existence of children's drawings, regardless of the forms they take, is advantageous for a living and minded being. As we have seen, children spontaneously regard drawing as play, and various authors have shown in detail how play, despite its appearance of disinterest, is a preparation for the practical activities of adulthood. Through the seriousness with which they go about drawing, and the faculties it involves, children forge, as it were, their own mental structure.

Turning now to the mental operations that contribute most to children's drawings, one is first struck by children's acute and spontaneous attention to things. This shows that realism is in accord with their conditions of existence, since in order to adapt to and dominate the environment, children clearly need to acquire as much detailed knowledge about it as possible.

The same conformity to the conditions of existence is also found in the fact that children initially are concerned with the totality and with the general, and only then with details and with what is individual. If they begin by grasping an object as a whole without distinguishing its different constituent elements, this is because it is as an entire object that any particular thing affords action. This passage from the general to the individual in mental development might at first seem implausible, since the inverse direction would seem to accord better with a certain *a priori* notion of the conditions of existence. In order to survive, it has been argued, children must be able to adapt to the environment and hence from the very outset they need to know about it as precisely as possible, in all its detail, so that they can coordinate their behaviour with the total complexity of each specific situation. Later on, having acquired some experience, they will then be able to notice that not all the characteristics of an object are of equal significance, and will differentiate those features which are essential from those which are rather incidental. Economy of effort, which optimises the use not only of physical but mental faculties, will then lead them to ignore the latter. But since at the outset of life children are unable to assess the relative importance of the different features of an object, they ought to have equal status for them. This is why children's drawings should be completely realistic from the very outset.

But the facts do not bear this out, and the facts must always come first. Why, then, this progression from the general to the particular, which seems to be at odds with the principle of finality? After all, it would surely be preferable to have a complete representation of every concrete case from the outset, not only for a purely contemplative mind, but even for a mind oriented to the practical. Now this would indeed be true if there were limitless available time. Unfortunately, the need to act cannot be postponed indefinitely, and a prompt decision is usually preferable to one that is well thought out but overdue. This is why a primitive creature has from the outset to be able to grasp only that which is important, and to know only that which concerns its activities. Admittedly, this will expose the creature to errors, by mistaking what is in fact incidental for what is important. There is the risk, then, of acting incorrectly. However, from the wider temporal perspective of the species, which is all that ultimately matters for the existence of its actual representatives, this possibility of error, that in extreme cases can lead to the death of the individual, is nevertheless more advantageous than any delay in acting caused by an incapacity to disregard what is incidental.

However, the importance of a character is a function of its generality, for the very simple reason that its degree of generality corresponds to the number of occasions it will be encountered in other objects. Thus the more general a character, the more informative it is about the future. A creature can only continue to survive at any time if it finds in the past indications for its present behaviour, and if, in turn, the present situation provides lessons for the future. But what lessons could be learnt from the purely individual, which, by definition, never occurs more than once? Thus, the more general a character, the greater the chances are that it will recur in new experiences, and the greater its biological significance. The reason that children's drawings initially neglect individual and transient characteristics derives from the same inevitable necessity that holds in life and in science. 'Research into the general' is the earliest and the most constant effort of the human mind, whereas aesthetic contemplation, which is oriented towards the individual, is only a luxury and for amusement. This is also why visual realism occurs after intellectual realism. What matters to the child is not the contingent and varying appearance of the object, dependent upon a particular viewpoint, but its appearance in itself, *sub specie aeternitatis*. Thus, even though drawing could be characterised from the child's perspective by its disinterestedness, it is no less the case that it is directed, from the outset, by practical utility and biological significance which either consciously or unconsciously dominate the whole of mental life.

The routine character of children's drawing, which is especially clear in the conservation of types or graphic techniques and in the fact that modifications made to some drawings are only gradually applied to others, is no less evidence of biological finality. Such routine, through its automatism, is just a particular case of habit, and it has the same advantages. Once the representation of established details of a motif have become fixed and automatic, attention is free to turn to new elements. Conservation of type is thus one of the preconditions for development, just as habit is a precondition for progress. Admittedly, if routine is preferable in some respects, it is also restrictive if it becomes routine in the strict sense. Yet, even so, automatism has a positive value. To abandon the old for the new constitutes progress if the new is an improvement on the old, but is otherwise a disadvantage. Furthermore, even when the new is better than the old, its superiority can only be appreciated following an experience carrying risks, and so it follows that remaining faithful to custom is usually more prudent, as far as the child is concerned. The new is unknown, whereas the old has been tested, and is at least manageable since it has, after all, brought the individual through to the present time. The old should only be relinquished gradually, and to the extent that the superiority of the new has been confirmed through extended experience. The histories of art, religion, politics, and society provide plenty of examples of commitment to custom comparable to conservation of type in children's drawings, and similar attempts to reconcile novelty and tradition analogous to the way children, when they introduce new details in their drawings, place them alongside older details that have been conserved.

Just as children conserve their own types and graphic conventions, they also insist that other people should conserve their ways of doing drawings for them. This rigid insistence has a well-known parallel in the way that children, when being told a story insist that it is told in exactly the same words, without any deviation, however trivial. This rigidity in circumstances of minimal importance is manifest more generally in their conduct, and demonstrates that instinct is their guide. They spontaneously find ways of doing things that a philosopher would also arrive at through reflection, based on strict deductions from the conditions of existence. The role of childhood is to allow the individual to acquire experience of life, and to learn how to act in a way most appropriate to the surrounding circumstances. The problem is reduced to its simplest terms when the circumstances remain fixed, since, in this case, the individual only has to repeat any behaviour that in identical circumstances had previously proved beneficial. However, if the circumstances vary, the individual must risk doing something without having any basis for anticipating whether the result will be positive or harmful. It is precisely for this reason that, in primary education, the child is put into a 'closed system', artificially isolated from excessively complicated and disturbing influences, just as one maintains a steady temperature in an incubator. It is a 'constant temperature' of this kind that children tend instinctively to maintain for themselves when they insist that a person who is telling a story always says it with the same words, or, when having a drawing done for them, must always have it drawn in the same way. They must have these rituals respected so that, when a certain person is going to tell them a story or draw them a picture, they know in advance what the story or drawing is going to be.

The purposiveness of children's instinctive activity also occurs in the curious phenomenon of 'duplicity of types' (see §29). Children arrive spontaneously at the most practical and appropriate ways of doing things. They have their own reasons, which they naturally regard as excellent, for drawing a certain subject according to a certain type. Nevertheless, they find that other people insist that they ought to draw that subject according to a different type, or else they assume they would prefer them to do so. As a consequence, children produce one type of drawing for themselves and a different type for other people. This is the same for their behaviour in general. They are told: do this, not that; stand straight; don't walk in the water. This is all well and good. They do not walk in the water in front of witnesses, and accept due reprimands and punishments when they misbehave. Yet they continue to walk in the water if they think they are not being observed. Hypocrisy? No: diplomacy, or opportunism. Outward allegiance to the law is not only reconcilable with the maintenance of individuality, but is even its precondition. In some cases at least, this duplicity of types is probably not just shrewd calculation, but, rather, politeness or sensitivity. Children may wish to give to the other person what they know or think they will like. And politeness being just an attenuated form of charity, perhaps that is what is involved here. Children do to others what they would wish to have done to themselves. Reasoning from their own case, they assume that other people share their same rigid commitment to sameness (i.e. conservation of type). Whatever the case may be, whether it is politics, politeness or altruism, it is always a social attitude that one finds in this characteristic of children's drawings. Here, as on other points, drawing casts light into the minds of children; we become witnesses of their first steps on the road of life, as apprentice adults.

One of the characteristics of children is the labile condition of their minds, or, to be more precise, the way their attention is fixed exclusively on the present moment, without any connection even to the immediate past. We have come across examples of such exclusive attention to the present, especially during the early years, in relation to their drawings: the principles of tacit correction; the difference between the interpretation given to the completed drawing and the initial intention which caused it to be drawn; the identity of their attitude towards their own drawings, the drawings of others, and actual objects; and, finally, synthetic incapacity, the spatial or else logical incoherence between different parts which have been drawn successively in the same drawing. Such lack of mental consistency has its disadvantages and would be very awkward if not corrected by its consequences. So why does this not occur from the outset? At the beginning, children still have not had time to accumulate sufficient experience to acquire those habits which would free their attention. Their attention has to be concentrated on what is essential, and what is essential is the present, since the present is the moment of action. The past is of interest only in so far as it continues into the present. Furthermore, the discontinuity between the past and the present is never absolute. Past and present are linked to one another by the association of ideas, which, as we have seen, constantly intervenes in drawings from the earliest age.

If the minds of children are closed to what is behind them, which has in a certain sense faded away, this is not the case for what is in front of them, for the future. And this is how it should be, since the individual in order to survive needs to live both in the present and for the future. Indeed, to the extent that the mind distances itself from the past, it can acquire greater flexibility regarding the future. If the association of ideas plays a large role in children's drawings, it should not, in most cases, be regarded as a mechanical process. To take just the example of association by resemblance, a resemblance between two objects or situations does not exist in itself, but only in relation to a mind capable of noticing it, and abstracting it from the differences that any resemblance always involves. Association by resemblance thus already implies a sense of analogy and serves as the basis of generalisation and imagination, both of which are indispensable for thought and action. Certainly, as we have seen for analogical transfer (§31–32), some analogies drawn by children can be mistaken; some of their imaginative creations are not viable; and, because of their lack of experience, their hypotheses are not always well founded. But hypothesis is an indispensable resource for both speculation and practical knowledge as long as its flights of fancy are subjected to correction through extended contact with reality. Otherwise, if the mind does not acquire circumspection, it remains inactive and incapable of progress.

Chance has a beneficial effect in children's drawings as in life more generally. I have already indicated how lucky accidents can help enrich the graphic repertoire of children. All development can be considered as the synthesis of two elements: an element of stability and one of progress. The first is none other than automatism or habit, the tendency to reproduce previous activities that have been successful. I have already discussed the role of automatism in children's drawings. But if this were the sole principle in human life there could be no progress. The individual would be able to conserve earlier acquisitions but incapable of any invention. Existence would be the perpetual reproduction of the same monotonous activities. But thanks to accidents, sometimes even mistakes by the agent, fortuitous or mechanical acts take on a new role or significance. An agent gifted with reflection notices a new function for an act which was earlier produced or distorted through accident, and thereby acquires new mechanisms adapted to different ends. Consequently, experience, or the effect of accidental external circumstances can provide an adequate explanation of the complexity of adult life, but with this one important proviso. We are not concerned with a subject, who, according to strict empiricism, is purely receptive, but with an agent endowed with reflection and capable of noticing new utility in either a fortuitous act or an established act distorted by chance, and who is able voluntarily to repeat the act and deliberately apply similar transformations to other acts and to other mechanisms established through acquired or hereditary automatism. It is through this process that, starting with instinctive movements and reflexes, human beings achieve, through the intermediary of secondary automatic reflexes such as speech or walking, the complex, novel and voluntary actions of adulthood.

Educational Implications

93. We have seen how drawing, as children engage in it, contributes to their mental development. But to what extent should education intervene in their spontaneous performance of this activity, and, if it should, how?

In relation to general education, I would go somewhat further than Rousseau, and his theory of non-intervention. Jean-Jacques failed to take account of the following two considerations. Those close to children are allowed to insist on conduct which, although annoying to children themselves, assures some peace for others, and they ought to do this if only to make children appreciate that society is actually part of their surrounding environment. It is also important to protect children from experiences that could prove harmful to them, such as climbing trees from which they might fall and hurt themselves. But these restrictions hardly apply to the special case of drawing.

I cannot accept unreservedly the doctrine of progressive education[27] that has become the latest word in education. Since school is an apprenticeship for life, it ought, in my view, to accustom children to the idea that life is not just a perpetual game. Children need to take on duties that may be irksome in themselves and nevertheless accept them for nothing but the satisfaction of doing them conscientiously and overcoming difficulties, since the advantage of such tasks lies in their effects, and in particular, the acquisition of skills of use in later life. But this function of establishing and exercising discipline is already satisfied by other aspects of school education which hold no attraction for the child. So they can be readily left to pursue their penchant for drawing, a form of play that is not only useful for its consequences, but even for the activity itself.

For these reasons, my advice, in connection with drawing, is for the educationalist to step aside, and let children draw what they want, proposing subjects if they need them, and, of course, if they ask for them. But they should not have subjects imposed on them, and above all they should be left to draw as they wish, in their own fashion.

One might think that the main advance that the educationalist could bring about would be to hasten advancement to the fourth stage, i.e. the substitution of intellectual realism by visual realism. But would this really be progress for the children themselves?

If civilised adults have largely become incapable of appreciating or even comprehending children's drawings, including even those they themselves once produced, it is also a well-established fact that not only savages, but even people with rudimentary culture are incapable of understanding drawings conforming to visual realism or photographs.[28] Furthermore, as we have seen, even civilised, 'well-washed' adults who are not themselves specially skilled in drawing continue to employ the techniques of children's drawings without any sense of embarrassment, even though they live in an

27. *'l'enseignement attrayant'*
28. In fact, much of the research claiming to show that 'uncivilised' people are unable to recognise the content of photographs or other perspectival pictures was inept, if not downright racist. See the excellent critical review by Rebecca Jones and Margaret Hagen, (1980), A perspective on cross-cultural picture perception, In M. Hagen (ed.), *The perception of pictures, Vol. II*. New York: Academic Press.

environment where visual realism is the only conception of representation acknowledged and practised.[29] Therefore there exists the same relation between visual and intellectual realism in relation to drawings as for different verbal languages, so that we could ask ourselves if intellectual realism should not be worthy of existing side-by-side with visual realism, just as Arabic exists alongside English. Indeed, 'grown-up' or skilful drawing conserves in certain circumstances and for special purposes something of the intellectual realism invented spontaneously by children. This is the case for anthropometric photographs with their double portrait of full-face and profile, and for architectural drawings with their elevation, plan, and various sections, which present in several contiguous images what children combine in a single image. There is the same concern to allow an observer to navigate mentally around the represented object and to penetrate into its interior. Furthermore engineers, mechanics, and designers also mix different points of view within the same drawing, just as children do.

With regard to graphic narration, we have seen how the symbolic type employed by adults and even the Epinal type are imperfect translations of change, in the way they combine identity and change. Only cinematography manages to reproduce change as such, but by an artificial technique, where the moving film presents at the same time the modification of changing elements and the permanence of unchanging ones. Yet, children's drawings of the successive type with repetition obtain pretty much the same result but with infinitely more economy, by numbering the different successive positions of the depicted changing elements on the unchanging background. Even this numbering is not essential, since the order of succession of the elements is clear enough, not only for the artist because of the order in which the elements were drawn, but also for anyone who knows the story being represented.

In short, visual realism is no less a convention than intellectual realism. Intellectual realism allows children's drawings to be, in their representation of space, a kind of flat sculpture (though sculpture, unlike children's drawings is not transparent), and, in their representation of time, a miniature theatre. It could thus be

29. Note that Luquet later in this same paragraph qualifies this statement in an important way. As he points out, there are many different kinds of representation, in addition to perspective, used even by expert illustrators and draughtsmen.

said to be a universal art, which at least merits serious examination before being dismissed.

Even if visual realism is preferred by adults, it seems to me that intellectual realism is more suitable for children. One of the universal roles rightly attributed to instruction in drawing is the development of the sense of observation. Now, by getting children to draw, one certainly attracts their attention to subjects in which they would not otherwise show much interest. Furthermore, the fact they have to create internal models, and retain and refine them, as their drawings develop, has important implications beyond drawing itself. Thus if one considers drawing as an element of 'object lessons', intellectual realism is infinitely better suited to this task than visual realism, precisely because it involves the depiction of all of the elements of the depicted object, each in its exemplary form, and in this way the child spontaneously engages in a kind of dissection of the object.

Hence there is no harm in leaving children to draw in intellectual realism, as they see fit, especially since, as we have seen, they will come in their own good time to prefer visual to intellectual realism. Any prescription imposed by others, even assuming children had developed sufficiently to understand it, would not be as effective as the obligation which they spontaneously impose on themselves once they have recognised the advantages of visual realism.

If nevertheless one should wish to hasten the graphic development of children, this is how in my view one ought to proceed. The most effective suggestions for children are those which are not made explicitly. The best way would be for adults to draw in front of them while making the same mistakes as they do, and talking out loud about the reasons for making corrections. For example, one might begin by drawing two eyes on a profile face, and then erase one of them while saying: 'Oh no! It should only have one eye: the other is on the side of the head and so cannot be seen.' Or else one might add a full-faced head to a body in profile, then show some hesitation and then stand in profile in front of the child and ask: 'Is his body like mine?' and when he or she replies 'yes', say 'And my head? Can you see two eyes? And the nose, is it in the centre of the head or at the edge?' and so on. In short, the teacher ought to put himself in the place of the child, yet also remain an adult for him or her so as to lead the child along with the teacher.

Needless to say, teachers, whether or not they wish to modify the spontaneous development of the child's drawings, need to take great care against errors of diagnosis. They should not automatically attribute the same significance to drawings produced by children that they might give to a similar drawing produced by themselves. All teaching, including that of drawing, should try to avoid misunderstandings between pupil and master. In order for the master to make himself understood by the child, he must first devote himself to understanding the child, which is in no way as simple as one might suppose.

Up until now, I have been talking about the domain in which any intervention by the teacher would be out of place. But there is another domain in which the teacher's instruction can be entirely worthwhile, and not at all insignificant. It is a fact that a great number if not the majority of children around the age of eleven completely lose any enjoyment in drawing to such an extent that they no longer continue with it. This sudden loss of interest in drawing is due, according to several educationalists, to the way in which they have been taught. I would rather say, to the way in which they have *not* been taught. It is true that children are put off certain activities for the sole reason that they are regarded as academic exercises. For example, at the level of secondary school teaching, a number of pupils are turned off our literary masterpieces because they are 'classics', or, in other words, 'works studied in class'. But I do not believe that this is the case for drawing. If children turn away from graphic activity, having once enjoyed it, it is not because they were made to draw at school, but because the way they were taught did not respect their aspirations, and, I have to say, their rightful aspirations. Children become disenchanted with drawing around the time they acquire the concept of visual realism and its fundamental commitment to perspective. The drawings in intellectual realism they used to produce no longer satisfy their now critical minds, but they feel incapable of producing drawings in the way they would now like. The aim of instruction therefore ought not to be to accelerate artificially the spontaneous development of drawing, and make children draw in visual realism when they still want to draw in intellectual realism, but rather to put them in the position of drawing effectively in visual realism once they have arrived at this intention.

Consequently, once children have manifested the desire for their drawings to conform to the visual appearance of things, it is appropriate to help them grasp the few main principles of perspective. Whereas verticals remain verticals, horizontals recede and become transformed into obliques, so that right angles become acute or obtuse. Circles take the form of ellipses which are either elongated in width or height. The dimensions of objects diminish with distance. More distant surfaces tend to be occluded by nearer ones. There is no need to resort to geometrical constructions to help the child understand perspective. One only has to show them these facts in relation to commonplace objects or events in their everyday experience. It is necessary to encourage them to draw as much as possible from nature, or, when this is not possible, to base their drawings on visual memories rather than intellectual constructions. In summary, since children now strive for resemblance in visual appearance, we should help them by educating their vision, and replacing the ingenuity that was once attached to intellectual realism.

After the conception, comes the performance. In addition to the education of the eye, there is also that of the hand. Taking into account both the requirements of drawing and the aspirations of the child, the aim is to teach the child to draw lines that correspond in shape and proportion as closely as possible to the object represented. This training in graphic movements, this development of technique, should certainly not be undertaken later than the practical instruction in perspective. But might it be possible to begin earlier, at the time when failed realism is giving rise to intellectual realism, or, in other words, from the beginning of primary school rather than kindergarten or nursery school? To answer this question properly, it would be necessary to conduct practical experiments that I have yet to do, and so I must restrict myself to setting out the psychological elements of the problem.

The fundamental point is that any intervention by the teacher should not destroy the child's spontaneous enjoyment of drawing. As we have seen, children are not only aware of the real shapes and proportions of the parts of objects even though they reproduce them incorrectly, but they occasionally even notice the mistakes in their drawings. They also have a taste for the regularity of lines. One might therefore respond to these spontaneous tendencies by helping them eliminate technical imperfections, which in any case decrease as children move beyond the stage of failed realism, and come to teach themselves how to draw lines which are no longer jagged, or circles which no longer look like potatoes.

But if such development of graphic ability seems only to offer advantages, there is a risk that the procedure that it requires could, if applied too soon, give rise to serious harm. After all, at least for rather novice adult artists, it seems that precise execution can only be obtained by proceeding with very short lines joined one to another. Furthermore, when making an initial sketch, artists use small tentative marks intended for later correction and only some of these are included in the final work after having been reworked and accentuated. But this runs completely counter to the way children do things. They draw freely in long strokes in single flourishes, so deep that the lines are almost engraved into the paper and may sometimes even scratch it, and when they make corrections they rely on tacit correction (ignoring rather than removing any unwanted lines). Now this spontaneous way of going about things is dictated by their concern to translate their mental representations onto paper as quickly as they can before they fade away. Since their attention is limited, the attention they devote to the production of the drawing may become diverted from its overall conception. All observers agree that concentration on the details can impair the whole, and that laboured execution of the drawing is a characteristic of backward and abnormal children. Premature attachment to graphic technique, which is merely a means, could totally disrupt the end, which is, after all, the *raison d'être* of technique. Training might enable the child to produce better executed lines, but the resulting representation might itself be poor. The remedy would then be worse than the disease, and the child, seeing the failings of the result, might be put off drawing altogether. Probably it would be better to engage in the correction of lines, and the procedures that involves, only in exercises in geometrical or ornamental drawing and decorative composition. The child might then, either spontaneously or through discrete suggestions, transfer the graphic technique thereby acquired to figurative drawings. But, once again, it will only be in the activity of instruction that teachers will be able to determine the practical value of this pedagogical hypothesis. In any case, as I see it, one thing is both certain and fundamental. No progress will be achieved by directly confronting head-on the spontaneous tendencies of children. Education should rather base itself upon those tendencies, and restrict itself to providing the means by which they may be better satisfied.

Short Bibliography

Barnes, Earl. (1896–1897). Children's pictures and stories. *Studies in Education, 1*. Stanford University.

Barnes, Earl. (1902). Studies in children's drawings. *Studies in Education, 2*. Philadelphia.

Brown, E.E. (1987). Notes on children's drawings. *University of California Publications in Education, 2*, 59–73.

Kerschensteiner, G. (1905). *Die Entwickelung der zeichnerischen Begabung*. Munich: K. Gerber.

Levinstein, S. (1905). *Kinderzeichnungen*. Leipzig: Voigtländer.

Lombardo-Radice, Giuseppe. (1925). Il disegno infantile, appunti di una madre. *L'educazione nazionale, 7*, 1–21.

Luquet, G.-H. (1913). *Les dessins d'un enfant: Thèse pour le doctorat presenté à la faculté des lettres de l'université de Lille*. Paris: Librarie Félix Alcan.

Luquet, G.-H. (1920). Les bonshommes têtards dans les dessin enfantin. *Journal de Psychologie, 17*, 680–710.

Luquet, G.-H. (1922). Genèse de l'art figuré: 1. La phase préliminaire du dessin enfanatin. *Journal de Psychologie, 19*, 695–719.

Luquet, G.-H. (1924). La narration graphique chez l'enfant. *Journal de Psychologie, 21*, 183–218.

Probst, M. (1906–1907). Dessins des enfants kabyles. *Archives de Psychologie, 6*, 130–40.

Rouma, G. (1913). *Le langage graphique de l'enfant* (2nd edn). Brussels: Mish and Thron.

Schreuder, A.J. (1902). Ueber Kinderzeichnungen. *Die Kinderfehler, 7*, 216–29.

Sully, J. (1895). *Studies of childhood*. London: Longman's, Green, and Co. French translation: *Etudes sur l'enfance*. Paris: F. Alcan, 1898.

Glossary of Key Terms

Alan Costall

Anthropocentrism (§46). Children tend to define objects according to their use (e.g. a chair is a 'to-sit-on'), and, Luquet argues, this emphasis upon the functional significance of objects is reflected in what they include and exclude in their drawings. Luquet's use of this term comes close to James Gibson's more recent concept of 'affordances'.

Colour (chapter 5). Children's use of colour in their drawings is a neglected topic of research, and Luquet's book still remains exceptional in providing an extended discussion, making a distinction between children's realist and decorative use of colour. He argues that children tend to use colour realistically when it is an intrinsic feature of the object: 'Colour is used decoratively when it is just an accidental feature of the represented object, that is, when it could exist in a different colour, as in the case of clothes. In contrast, it is realistic when the colour is essential to the object' (§50).

Designated object (§17). The object named by the child when giving an interpretation to the drawing.

Duplicity of type (§29). 'Children not only recognise that other people draw according to types different from their own, ... but, furthermore, when they are drawing for someone else, will adopt the types of that other person instead of their own.' In other words, children are not only aware that there are different ways of drawing something, but may draw one type for themselves and another for other people.

Exemplarity (§§42 and 47). The treatment of a specific object as a generic representation of objects of that kind, e.g. a particular person as representative of people in general.

Exemplarity of form (§§79, 87). A specific object and its details drawn so that its shape and essential features are most conspicuous and characteristic. Other writers have used the term 'canonical form' to convey a similar concept.

Failed realism (chapter 8). Following the stage of 'fortuitous realism' the child attempts to create realistic drawings on purpose, but lacks both the skill and ability to attend to each part of the drawing in relation to the whole.

Fortuitous realism (chapter 7). Resemblances produced, not deliberately, but in the course of making traces for their own sake. The child, noticing these fortuitous resemblances, begins to make deliberate small changes to improve the resemblance, and eventually begins to try to produce such overall resemblances deliberately.

Graphic automatism (§12). The very act of drawing a particular subject may lead to perseveration, so that the same subject may be drawn over and over again by the child. These drawings may be produced in a single sitting, as it were, or spread over the course of several days. This tendency can also lead to the repetition of details within a drawing (§32).

Graphic narration (chapter 10). Drawings of events or changing scenes (see also §47). Children use one of three techniques:

1. The symbolic type: 'The selection of just one phase of the action or episode of the story as the most important, and using this as a symbol of the entire event' (§81).
2. The Epinal type: This type 'does not represent the story by a single image symbolising the entire event, but instead there are several complete images each depicting one of the moments, and sufficing in itself to represent the corresponding episode, just as the single image of the symbolic type represents the entire event. This is the technique used in *Epinal* images [early colour strip cartoons]' (§82).
3. The successive type: 'Unlike the Epinal type, but just like the symbolic type, it includes a single image. But whereas each of the constituent images of the Epinal type only contains elements that could be seen at any one time, this third type of graphic narration combines elements which objectively belong to different moments of the event or, to be more precise, elements which could only be seen in succession' (§83). There are two variants, one where the elements are *repeated* whenever they do something different or something different happens to them, and one where each item is represented just once in relation to one episode in the event (§84).

Intellectual realism (chapter 9). In contrast to visual realism, the aim of intellectual realism is to represent the object 'in itself' rather than just those details that can be seen from a single perspective. 'The very essence of intellectual realism is to depict all of the constituent elements of the object represented.'

Intention (chapter 1). The idea the child has in mind when embarking on a representational drawing, and which motivates the child to try to represent a specific subject.

Internal model (§34). According to Luquet, drawings corresponding to intellectual realism are based, not on the visual appearance of the object, but on the child's mental representation of all its salient features.

Interpretation (chapter 2). The child's description of the drawing after it is drawn, e.g. 'it's a frog'. The interpretation does not necessarily correspond to the original intention for the drawing, and may even be applied to drawings that initially had no representational intention at all.

Motif. By 'motif', Luquet means the subject of the drawing, such as a man, animal, or house.

Plan (§75). 'Showing the object projected onto the ground surface, ... like a bird's eye view'.

Productive mistakes (§21). As a result of children's limited skill, their drawings do not always turn out as they intended, but lend themselves, instead, to different interpretations. This leads children to try out new subjects, thus enhancing their repertoire.

Rabattement or folding-out (§76). 'An absolutely impossible kind of perspective ... a procedure which is applied from the outset to the supports and also vertical features of objects, such as the feet and legs of animals and furniture and the wheels of vehicles. This involves folding out each of the supports as though they were connected to the object by hinges around which they can be turned.' This technique is used for any feature of an object that might otherwise be occluded.

Realism (chapter 6). The aim 'to provide the most faithful and complete representation of the object' (§78). According to Luquet, realism takes two distinct forms: intellectual and visual realism.

Stage theory. An explanation of development that postulates a series of distinct stages through which the child progresses. Although

Luquet's account of the development of drawing is widely regarded as a stage theory, he repeatedly reminds the reader that the different modes of representation he identifies are not mutually exclusive, and indeed may coexist in a single drawing even for adults (e.g. §88).

Synthetic incapacity (§67). The failure to coordinate the various parts of a drawing into a coherent whole, both in terms of the spatial relations between them and also their logical relationships. The failure arises not only from limited skill in drawing, but also from the inability, during the act of drawing, to hold more than one detail of the drawing in mind at any one time. According to Luquet, this failure 'is the essential characteristic of the stage of failed realism'.

Tacit correction. Sometimes when children have made a mistake and added a correction, they do not explicitly cross out or erase the incorrect lines, but simply act as though the initial incorrect detail were no longer there.

Tadpole men. Drawings of people in which 'the trunk is absent, so that the arms, if they are shown, have to be attached either to the legs or, more often, to the head' (§23 *et seq.*).

Trace making (chapter 7). The making of marks purely for its own sake, without any intention of creating a resemblance to something else.

Transfer by analogy (§§ 11 and 31). Analogy based on visual appearance, giving rise to a new intention for a drawing: 'There are two distinct forms: in the first case, the resemblance is based on the appearance of the *objects* depicted, in the second it is based on their *representation*.' On the basis of such analogies, the child may transfer details or even the overall 'type' associated with one object to that of another. For example, children carry over to their earliest drawings of animals the details and even the overall form of their drawings of people.

Transparency (§74). The depiction of 'details which would otherwise occlude other elements as if they were transparent, thus allowing the other elements to be seen'.

Type. 'The *way* in which any given child represents the same object or motif over a sequence of drawings, shows a gradual development. It is the result of two factors, an element of stability (conservation of the type), and an element of change (modification of the type)' (§22).

Visual realism (chapter 9). According to this system of representation, a drawing must be 'a kind of photograph of the object, reproducing all those details, but only those details, which can be seen from where the object is viewed, and with the shape they project from that viewpoint: in short, the object has to be depicted in perspective' (§71). Note that the term 'perspective' can mean, at one extreme, the full-blown use of linear perspective, and, at the other, simply the omission of an occluded feature (such as, 'the representation of a single eye in profiles of heads'). Luquet often fails to distinguish these diffferent senses, as does much of the modern literature on children's drawings.

Index

analogy of shape, 23
anthropocentrism, 58, 156
Arnheim, Rudolph, x, xii–xiii, xxi n.15
association of ideas, 13–7, 40
associationism, 142
autism, xii, xx n.6

Baldwin, James Mark, 87–8
Bühler, Karl, xi

captions, 104–5
change of viewpoint, 115–22, 156
colour, 65–73, 156
Comte, Auguste, xxii n.19, 142
correction of drawing, 6–7, 164
Cubism, xv, xvii, xx, xxi n.16

designated object, 19, 162
disenchantment with drawing, 158
drawing techniques, xv, 105–23
duplicity of types, 37–8, 151–2, 162

educational implications, 157–60
empiricist theory of development, 144–7
Epinal type of graphic narration, 130–1, 137–8, 163
exemplarity, 53, 162
exemplarity of form, 62–4, 102, 162
experimental studies, viii

failed realism, 93–101, 163
fortuitous realism, 85–92, 163
Freeman, Norman, xxi n.9

Galton, Francis, 56
generic images, 53
graffiti, xx n.2, 38
graphic automatism, 14–16, 41–2, 163
graphic homonymy, 7 fig.4, 17 fig.11
graphic narration, xvii, 58 fig.53, 63–4, 129–40, 156, 163
graphic puns, 26

Hagen, Margaret, xxi n.17, 155 n.28
human figure drawings 36, 46, 57–62, 81, 83, 94, 99, 103, 120; *see also* split profile, tadpole men

idealism, 78, 83–4
imitation, 86–7
incompatible details, 23–4
inhibition, xiii, xxi n.8
innocent eye, ix–xiii, xx n.5
intellectual realism as a choice, xvii
intellectual realism, xiii–xviii, 47–8, 102–28, 138–9, 141, 156, 163–4
intention, 3–17, 164

internal model, xiv–xv, 19, 47–64, 164
interpretation, 18–30, 52, 77–8, 164
interpretation, conflict with intention, 21

Jones, Rebecca, xxi n.17, 155 n.1

Kant, Immanuel, 4

logical realism, xxi n.10
loss of interest in drawing, 158

Matthews, John, xxii n.18
methods of study, vii–viii, xx n.2
models, role of, 12–13, 39–40, 48–51, 65
morphological analogy, 13–14
motif, choice of, 8–9, 51, 164
multiplication of details, 41–3

orientation, 100

perspective, x, xvi, xxi n.14, xxii n.21, 102, 158–9, 166
plan views, 109–10, 164
Preyer, Wilhelm, x
primitive art, 142
productive mistakes, 30, 164

rabattement, 55 fig.52, 110–15, 164
Read, Henry, xxi n.15
realism, xxi n.12, 77–84, 122, 141, 148, 164
Rousseau, Jean-Jacques, 154

schematism, 83
scribbling, xxii n.18, 3
split profile, 34
stage theory, xvi–xviii, 164–5
stages as continuous and coexisting, 91–2, 100–1, 125, 142
successive type of graphic narration, 131–7, 163
Sully, James, ix–x
symbolic type of graphic narration, 129–30, 137, 163
synthetic incapacity, 95–101, 141, 165

tadpole men, 15
teasing, 25–6
trace making, 85–7, 165
transfer by analogy, 40, 165
transparency, 108–9, 165
type, 31–46, 165

value of child art, xix–xx
visual realism, use in early childhood, xxii n.21, 37, 124–5
visual realism, 123–8, 138–40, 141, 166